OFFICIAL

ZORK™

GRAND INQUISITOR
MARGARET STOHL

STRATEGY GUIDE

////BradyGAMES

LEGAL STUFF

BRADY PUBLISHING

An Imprint of
Macmillan Digital Publishing
201 West 103rd Street
Indianapolis, Indiana 46290

ISBN: 1-56686-721-5

Library of Congress Catalog No.: 97-74062

Printing Code: The rightmost double-digit number is the year of the book's printing; the rightmost single-digit number is the number of the book's printing. For example, 97-1 shows that the first printing of the book occurred in 1997.

00 99 98 97   4 3 2

Manufactured in the United States of America.

Acknowledgments

I acknowledge Debra McBride, from Brady, who is my friend and who gave all this Zorkanalia a home.

I acknowledge Matt Harding, (designer on ZGI) my co-collaborator on all things related to Zork—along with co-conspirators Ted Peterson (designer on ZGI) and Laird Malamed (director of ZGI and my friend from third grade). Thanks, Thanks, and Thanks.

I acknowledge Cecilia Barajas, who directed *Zork Nemesis,* and who invited me into the Underground in the first place. (And Natasha Paola Barajas Lasky, who is her boss.) Thanks.

I acknowledge Elizabeth Storz, Mason Deming, Mike Douglas, Yasmin Salas, David Dalzell, Eni Oken, Huisok Pyon, Christian Astillero, Will Westwater, Scott Lahman, and the rest of the super talented creative productive neurotic forces behind *Zork Grand Inquisitor*. Thanks.

I acknowledge Lewis, Emma and May Peterson as my super talented creative productive neurotic family. Thanks.

To my Activision friends, I say only this (if you haven't figured it out by now): The Spice is the Worm! The Worm is the Spice!

If you want to contest, correct, or corroborate anything, or know more about Zork, email Laird Malamed, who directs the Zork Franchise, at zork@activison.com.

BRADY GAMES STAFF

Publisher
Lynn Zingraf

Editor-in-Chief
H. Leigh Davis

Title/Licensing Manager
David Waybright

Marketing Manager
Janet Cadoff

Acquisitions Editor
Debra McBride

CREDITS

Project Editor
David Bartley

Copy Editor
Howard Jones

Screen Shot Editor
Michael Owen

Book/Cover Designer
Scott Watanabe

Production Designer
Dan Caparo

TABLE OF CONTENTS

ZORK™ GRAND INQUISITOR

Introduction

Above all else, Zork has a history... twenty years of history.

In many ways, the history of Zork is the history of the game indust—

Wait a minute. Is Starbuck really in this game? That guy from the A-Team?

Dirk Benedict? Yeah, that macrobiotic, cigar-smoking, line-rewriting stud. But as I was saying, the early Zork games, Infocom text adventures, evolved in the wake and style of "Adventure," and became remembered as some of the first computer games ever...

And that guy who throws the confetti? With the twirly moustache? That guy from Hollywood Squares?

That's Rip Taylor. Yeah. He's hilarious and we thought it would be a genre-busting piece of performance art to see him in a game... and... I've totally lost my place.

You were saying something about Zork.

I got it. Thanks.

Don't mention it.

When Zork became graphical with the popular *Return to Zork*, it was released as one of the few pioneering titles for the CD-ROM, a newly-evolving platform.

And Lenny and Squiggy? Lenny's that Spinal Tap guy, right?

That's right. Throughout it all, Zork games have enjoyed twenty years of high adventure and low cunning, good nature and bad puns...

But you never hear about Carmine, do you?

I'm just going to ignore that.

I wonder what happened to the Big Ragu?

Zork Grand Inquisitor gleefully embraces this spirited non-sensibility, and showcases many of the creatures and environments of the past twenty years of...

Is this almost over? If I read this any longer the guy at the counter is going to make me buy the book. Where's the stuff I need to know?

That would be the walkthrough. The beginning section of the walkthrough explains the basic interface of the game, then it breaks down every section of the game by environment, first giving hints for puzzle solving, then solutions. Because this is an inventory-based game, you will be carrying objects that you find in one area of the game with you to complete puzzles all over the underground. To help you keep track of what you're finding and where you found it, each section of the walkthrough also details objects found and taken.

But wait, there's more.

It slices, it dices—no, really, I was listening.

   This book contains just about everything cool there is to know about *Zork Grand Inquisitor*. Confused by one of the (parallel) universe's only non-chronological histories? Check out Chapter Six. Interested in the famous faces that pop up all over the game? Refer to Chapter Two, ZGI's (To-Use-The-Term-Literally) Characters. More of a story person? Read through Chapter Three, the detailed backstory of *Zork Grand Inquisitor*, and find out how the Dungeon Master and the Grand Inquisitor met at GUE Tech. A card-collecting, mana-lovin' magic freak? Read about the Treatise of Magic in Chapter Five.

Who are you calling a freak, man?

   Did I mention Starbuck is in this game?

Cool.

CHAPTER I: THE STORY

You begin *Zork Grand Inquisitor* as a luckless adventurer—your standard nameless-age-less-faceless-gender-neutral-culturally-ambiguous-adventure-person, to be exact. With not a zorkmid in your knapsack, and little idea of what lies ahead, you find yourself wandering about the historic town of Port Foozle. Port Foozle has seen better days; as you wander through the town…

Mir Yannick, the Grand Inquisitor of Zork, has parlayed his position as the head of the mega-conglomerate Frobozz Electric to rule the land like a fascist regime. Because Frobozz Electric owns all patented technology in the land, as long as the Inquisition can keep magic from the people, the inquisition can rule the populace as they please. And how they please, it turns out, is not so pleasant at all.

The story of *Zork Grand Inquisitor* quickly becomes the story of the quest (yours) to return magic to the deprived Empire. But you must act fast—the Grand Inquisitor has a plan, a super-plan (don't they always, those dastards!) that will tighten his grip on the minds of the Quendorans so painfully, that it might never be reversed. You have one day before he unleashes his own personal death star on the Empire—a powerful mind-control device, in the form of the Inquisition Cable Network, INQUIZIVISION. With Inquizivision, non-stop twenty-four-hours-a-day Inquisition programming will brainwash the already mind-numbed, dogma-fed population until their brains will become useless mush.

But you soon discover why the Grand Inquisitor is attempting to tighten his stranglehold now. He's growing more nervous by the day because strange occurrences—rumors of supernatural sightings—are talked of with increasing clamor by the populace. The Grand Inquisitor fears a magic rebellion growing from the people. And his fears are founded in truth; magic, in a fundamentally magic land, cannot be banished forever, and all about you magical things really do seem to be struggling to return to their magical lives.

Luckily, you aren't alone in your quest. With a bit of good fortune, you stumble across what appears to be an old, battered brass lamp. (It's in a crate marked "Infocom," and appears to be a classic adventurer's lamp, bequeathed to you from your adventuring forebearers of text-adventures past.)

You soon find that magic isn't gone, but has been forced underground. A glimmer of hope remains in the form of the disenchanted Dungeon Master, Dalboz of Gurth, who has been banished by the Grand Inquisitor. He will become a powerful ally on your quest. Actually, he has no choice but to become your ally, as he's stuck inside your lamp, and accompanies you along your quest.

FACTOID

Throughout this book, we will reprint some of the material from the Zork Grand Inquisitor Design Document. The Design Document is the bible, blueprint and very large treatise upon which the game is based. It is used by the production team to keep track of everything, the testers to make sure it is all there when we release the game, and the money people to leave unread on their shelves when they green-light a project. In any event, the design changes from time to time, so occasionally you will read a description that does not exactly match what appears on screen. Relax, we won't steer you off-course. What you are experiencing is the transformation from written idea to realized game. It is perfectly safe.

Though the Dungeon Master can no longer practice magic, he can help you advance in your own knowledge of the supernatural arts. With his help, you may even gain a spell book and fill it with contraband spells that have been hidden throughout the empire, in hopes of spiriting some magic away from the Inquisition. Together, you contact the enchantress Y'Gael, a familiar Zork character who has in times past led the Enchanters' Guild to hide all of Known Magic in the Empire into a powerful relic known as the Coconut of Quendor. If the Coconut could be recovered, along with the two other most powerful artifacts in Zork's magic treasury—a Cube of Foundation and the Skull of Yoruk—magic would again flow through Zork. And it is here your quest begins in earnest. You must reclaim the lost treasures of Zork.

You soon meet up with three other traveling companions who wish to (well, okay, have no choice but to) join your quest. All three are one-time magical creatures who have been stripped of their magic faculties and imprisoned in flat, metal disks called Totems. The Grand Inquisitor, who possesses a fearsome machine called the Totemizer, continues to victimize magical creatures with this technology. One day he hopes to have utterly "cleansed" the land of any remaining traces of magic.

The three Totems that come to help with your quest include the beautiful and telepathic Lucy Flathead, one of the only remaining descendants of the House of Flathead that once ruled the Empire; the thick-witted, all-brawn no-brain Brogmoid "Brog," who is something like a cross between a troll and Chewbacca; and the whiny, neurotic Griff, who suffers a Dragon inferiority complex and wants desperately to avoid physical pain. Together, you form an unlikely band of Adventurers who join forces to—with any luck—recover the lost treasures, destroy the Grand Inquisitor, and finally return magic to its rightful place in the Empire.

And who knows? Perhaps even return the rightful heir to the throne…

(For a more in depth accounting of the story leading up to the gameplay of Zork Grand Inquisitor, see the "Backstory" section of this book which is covered in Chapter Three.)

Chapter II:
The Characters

...And They Are Characters, All Right!

The characters and creatures of *Zork Grand Inquisitor* are a wacky bunch, to say the least. Many of the personalities in the game are returning figures from the last twenty years of the Zork series—Belboz and the Dungeon Master (*Zork I,II,III*), the Grand Inquisitor (*Nemesis*), Y'Gael (*Enchanter Trilogy*), and of course, the Empire has always boasted Flatheads and Brogmoids, Dragons and Grues, Flickering and Bickering Torches.

But even the familiar favorites have a new look in ZGI, which is the first Zork game to employ modeled CG characters, giving life to a few of the more wildly imaginative creatures of the universe. Hallelujah! For the first time in twenty years, we can see for ourselves what the creatures of Zork look like. Now, if we could only catch a glimpse of the Grue...

And, in the retro spirit of the twenty year anniversary of the series, *Zork Grand Inquisitor* has even extended its classically wacky non-sensibility to the casting of the live-action video portion of the game, as well. The cast includes a few popular culture icons from the past twenty years—not to mention a few amazing characters of their own accord. This is by far my favorite cast of any FMV in any game I've seen to date.

The Dungeon Master

The Third Dungeon Master, or Dalboz of Gurth, once ruled over magic in the Underground.

Factoid

Throughout the Zork Trilogy (Zork One, Two, Three) the Player trains to become the second Dungeon Master, which happens at the end of Zork Three. At the end of Zork Zero, the Player becomes the first Dungeon Master. In Zork Grand Inquisitor, Dalboz is the Third Dungeon Master. If you successfully complete the game, you become the Fourth.

However, since the end of magic in the empire, the Dungeon Master became just about the boss of nothing. Now, thanks to the Grand Inquisitor and the newly patented Frobozz Electric Anti-Magic Repellent ("Kills Wizards, Dead!") the Dungeon Master is merely a disembodied voice crammed into the player's lantern.

Factoid

In Return to Zork, the player was accompanied by the Wizard Tremble, another disembodied voice crammed in a crystal ball. He made his dazzling appearance on the scene with the now hallowed line "I need a new battery." Eddie Dombrower, (a.k.a. the Wizard Tremble) who led the Return to Zork team, is now an executive at Henson Productions with the Muppets.

The Dungeon Master functions as the sidekick or buddy to the player, crabbing at what befalls the two of them, trying to remember how he became a disembodied voice, trying to help restore magic to the Empire—and himself to his body. In a world where magic has gone "underground," the Dungeon Master has become the de facto leader of the magic counterculture. It is his companionship and advice that helps the Player restore Magic to the Empire.

The voice of the Dungeon Master in *Zork Grand Inquisitor* is played by Michael McKeon, who has starred in *Laverne and Shirley*, *This is Spinal Tap*, and *The Brady Bunch Movie*, among other projects. His girlfriend gave him *Zork Nemesis* for Christmas last year.

FACTOID

People are always either banishing or restoring magic to the Great Underground Empire (GUE). In Spellbreaker, the evil doppelganger of the head of the circle of enchanters banishes magic in 966 GUE. In Zork Grand Inquisitor, magic (hopefully) returns in 1067 GUE. Magic returns in Return to Zork in 1647 GUE. It's sort of a franchise thing.

THE GRAND INQUISITOR

Mir Yannick, or the Grand Inquisitor, is leader of the anti-magic Inquisition, and CEO of Frobozz Electric.

The Grand Inquisitor is your basic bad guy corporate type who hates the magic counter-culture and the touchy-feely "peace love magic" freedom lovers who espouse magic. He is an evil, sarcastic, even bored dictator who loves—and loves owning—technology. He is the beneficiary of a long-life spell that was cast upon him hundreds of years ago by his one-time classmate Dalboz of Gurth (the Dungeon Master).

Yannick plans to inflict pain on the people of the Empire for an eternity. He pretends to be the religious leader of the land as a means of obtaining power—but he's really not interested in anything except the technologies he employs to make certain he will forever rule the Empire. Inquizivision, the Inquisition Cable Network, is the diabolical tool by which he plans to realize his dastardly dreams. He progresses in anger and irritability as he nears your capture.

FACTOID

The Grand Inquisitor made his first appearance in Zork Nemesis, where, if you looked on the front door of Steppinthrax Monastery, you could see a proclamation explaining that it was closed by order of the Grand Inquisitor.

FACTOID

Refer to the Backstory for the narrative of this tidy bit of unfortunate spellcasting.

The Grand Inquisitor is played by Eric Avari, whose feature credits include *Stargate*, *Independence Day*, and *Encino Man*, to name a few. The next time Eric leads an Inquisition, I expect he will decree as first order of business that the Inquisition Personnel wear anything other than long-sleeved wool military jackets on hot Green Screen sound stages.

Antharia Jack

Antharia Jack is the
Indiana Jones of the Empire.

This washed-up Adventurer isn't just an Adventurer, he's an Adventurer from Zork's own "Great Underground Adventure" series—not to mention the smash hit, the "Z-Team." As the game progresses, Jack becomes intertwined with the player's own goals and trajectories; some of the player's puzzles affect how Jack is treated in the cut scenes throughout the game.

Ultimately, Jack searches out and reunites with his long lost love, one of the totems, Lucy Flathead. He finds his own love, decides to do his own stunts, and in his own way, becomes an Adventurer of sorts. This game becomes his big comeback vehicle, so to speak.

There's a new Adventurer in town—Antharia Jack is back.

The role of Antharia Jack is played by Dirk Benedict, probably best known to Zork fans as the stogie-smoking Starbuck from *Battlestar Galactica*, and of course, Face from *The A-Team*. Recently on screen in *Alaska*, Dirk lives in Montana with his two sons.

Chief Undersecretary Wartle

Chief Undersecretary Wartle, the irritating, mustachioed second-in-command of the Magic Inquisition, is the effervescent minion, henchman, and confidante of the more bile-ridden Grand Inquisitor. Wielding his remote control, Wartle leads the Inquisition Guard through Port Foozle with all the bravado of... of... Rip Taylor.

The role of Chief Undersecretary Wartle was played by Rip Taylor, who has starred in a million things, but is perhaps best remembered for his role in *Hollywood Squares*. He lives in Vegas and, more than that, he is Vegas.

Factoid

A fabulous oil painting of Rip hangs enshrined in the Debby Reynolds Casino, a remarkable establishment that is now sadly threatened with bankruptcy.

Factoid

Actual confetti was ruled out of the game, as it would have been too hard to composite. We like to feel that Confetti is rather somehow implied by the mere presence of the Chief Undersecretary.

Factoid

Rip Taylor treated the cast and crew of Zork Grand Inquisitor to a soulful rendition of "I Saw Elvis Outside the Piggly-Wiggly."

THE GRIFF

The Griff is a neurotic, whiny cross between a runt dragon and a small winged lion.

The Griff is principally defined by his neuroses and fears—which are numerous, but include a crushing fear of heights that makes flying difficult, if not impossible. He has a rather extreme dragon inferiority complex, and spends a lot of time and wit haranguing the muddle-brained Brog—the two are friends, if opposites. Above all, he tries to avoid pain, discomfort, and heroic actions of any kind. His highly-developed superego keeps these basic tenets of adventuring in check. The voice of the Griff is played by Marty Ingels, the skilled comedian whose credits include The Pac-Man Animated series.

FACTOID

The id, the ego, and the superego are the three parts of the individual psyche, as defined by Sigmund Freud. Freud died on September 23, 1939. Which is 37 years and 244 days before Star Wars was released.

FACTOID

Pac-Man aired in 1982, five years after Star Wars was released.

FACTOID

Marty and Shirley were married in 1977, allowing us to add them to the 20 year old franchise list.

FACTOID

Marty Ingels is married to Shirley Partridge and is thus the step-father of David Cassidy. Marty Ingels once collected enough pocket change from around the house to total one million dollars. David Cassidy now has his own show in Vegas. If you miss his show, the billboard says, you missed Vegas.

LUCY FLATHEAD

This beautiful, sexy, telepathic Flathead—one of the only known Flathead descendants in the Empire—has been imprisoned as a totem because of her anti-Inquisition political activism. Lucy is one of the three totems, like inanimate chess pieces, who travel with the player and the Dungeon Master throughout the game. She is logical, intelligent, witty, scathing, and a bit defensive. She thinks she is always right and usually is. The Dungeon Master thinks she's a pain in the ass and she usually is. She's our girl Spock. In spite of her iron will, she falls in love with Antharia Jack. You go girl.

The role of Lucy Flathead is played by Amy Jacobson, who numbers among her credits *The Big Easy* (cable) and who knows how to fire some big guns. She looks good even in a flat head, which says something about what she looks like in her round head.

"BROG" THE BROGMOID

The Brog is a squat, hairy, troll-type beast that is absolutely every bit as strong as he is stupid. The Brog loves to pick up rocks, smash rocks, throw rocks, and of course, eat rocks. His favorite color is rocks. His favorite game is rocks. His best friends are rocks. Though Brogs are generally short, hairy fellows, this Brog is a Brogmoidus Domesticus—a rare blue hairless Brog. In the course of this game, the big-hearted Brog will quite possibly become intensely loyal to you and your mates. Just think of him as a very stupid, very small Chewbacca. In a leopard skin Speedo.

FACTOID

Earl Boen had never been exposed to the poem novella "Green Eggs and Ham" prior to this recording session. As with all the voice-over actors, Earl was skillfully directed by Chris Zimmerman, who trained as a cartoon director at Hanna Barbara (Johnny Quest), before becoming a freelance voice director. And what major movie star did she direct doing voice overs for a cartoon? You guessed it. Bruce Willis.

The voice of the Brog was played by Earl Boen, whose voice-over credits include *Bruno The Kid* and *The Real Adventures of Johnny Quest*. Earl Boen is also the voice of the Inflatable Sea Captain.

The Enchantress Y'Gael

Y'Gael is the beautiful, lost enchantress of the Enchanters' Guild. She was last seen with the Coconut of Quendor as she sailed away on the Great Sea to preserve all magic for another time and place. She orients the Adventurer at two critical junctures in the quest, awarding the player a spellbook at the onset, and offering some final, critical words before the last puzzle of the game.

Y'Gael is a bit spacey (well, she has been spending 100 years in the deep "space" of the parallel existence). She's also a part of the Magic Counterculture, and acts the mellow "peace love magic" freedom' fightin' part.

She represents the magic that must be, and ultimately is, saved and returned to the land.

The role of Y'Gael was played by Jordana Capra, who has also been featured in the television series *Night Stand*.

FACTOID

This actor was apparently considered for the sequel to the Best selling Adventure Game of All Time, except they ultimately felt her to be "too urban;" they were going for this ethnic, mystic thing. I hear that's what they told Rip Taylor as well.

Floyd the Bouncer (in Jack's Speakeasy)

Tough and big, but goofy looking, Floyd the Bouncer keeps all the low-lifes in and the respectable folk out of Jack's Speakeasy, back in time in Old Port Foozle.

You might recognize Don Gibb, who played Floyd, as "Ogre" from *Revenge of the Nerds*, among other roles. We know we did.

The Two-Headed Guardian of Hades

Cerebus is the three-headed dog, right? This two-headed guardian of the doorway to Hell is just a temp, sent from an agency, just punching the clock like you and me. Perhaps this accounts for the loss of one head from the motif.

The voices of the two Heads are played by Chick Venerra, who has done more than a few famed cartoon voices on *Johnny Quest* and *Animaniacs*.

Marvin the Mythical Goatfish

Marvin the Mythical Goatfish lives under the dock at Foozle. He's lucked into a bit of sunken magical treasure—and is more than paranoid that you're fishing for it. Not to mention personally offended, as a fish.

The voice of Marvin the Goatfish was played by Roger Rose, a very funny voice talent who also does voices for *Johnny Quest*.

Factoid

One of the cut scenes from the live-action of Zork Grand Inquisitor included the torture of said Goatfish, the eventual cleaning and gutting that climaxed with the Bravehearted fish crying out "Freeeedom!"

Voice of the Inquisition Propaganda in Port Foozle

That voice. That grating, whining, nerdy announcer voice. You just can't turn it off in Port Foozle, and it will drive you nutty until you solve that puzzle. That voice might sound familiar to you; it's played with smarm and style by David Lander, T.V.'s historical and hysterical "Squiggy," from *Laverne and Shirley* and a host of other film, voice

over, and feature work. He also has this really great watch that tells you all the baseball scores of all the games that are happening, everywhere in the country. David is also the voice of the Bickering Torch.

Inquisition Guard

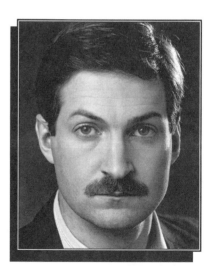

This guard shadows Chief Undersecretary Wartle when he harrasses you, and Antharia Jack, and Lucy Flathead, and the Griff, and of course all the good citizens of Port Foozle. He's a bit starstruck by Antharia Jack, and loves to smite anybody he gets a chance to. There's nothing like a good bit of smitation, though, Chief Wartle will tell you that much.

The Inquisition Guard is played with aplomb by Oliver Muirhead, whom we recognized from the Tombstone Pizza commercials. What do you want written on your Tombstone?

THE INSPECTOR

The Inspector is the Monty Python-esqe type character Antharia Jack (and you) meet up with at the Totemizer. He's actually a lamb, really—very friendly and supportive, considering he's about to render you an inanimate object. And he's got an amazing right hook, as Jack comes to learn for himself.

The Inspector is played by Douglas Carrigan, who has a lengthy list of theatrical credits and who hit it off with Dirk Benedict as if they were about to become the next Laurel & Hardy or Abbott & Costello.

THE BARTENDER

"Want Some Rye?!" The Bartender is played with over-powering style by Earl Schuman, who lists *Seinfeld* in his credits and has lots of stories about how nice all those Seinfeld people are. Come to think of it, he has lots of stories, in general. He's a real charmer. And those are, in fact, his own glasses.

THE SIX-ARMED INVISIBLE BRIDGE GUARD

Pants! Now! If it's not Scottish, it's Crap! The Six-Armed Invisible Bridge Guard used to be the Six Armed Purple Bridge Guard, clearly,

until somebody used the IGRAM (Turn Purple Things Invisible) Spell on him. The S.A.I.B.G. is a formidable opponent until you learn what it takes to disarm him.

The voice of the S.A.I.B.G. is played by Donovan Freberg, son of radio star Stan Freberg, and well-known in the world of voice actors in his own right. And he even likes video games. Donovan Freberg is also the voice of Doug, on the Dungeon Master's Answering Machine.

SNEFFLE THE BAKER
(OR THE MAN WHO LIVES
IN THE DRAGON'S THROAT)

Shipwrecked when his ship was wrecked, so to speak, in the mouth of the WatchDragon of the Great Sea, Sneffle is

never one, you know, not to make the best of things. Although he does live in the throat of a Dragon, and can never return to his bakery, he certainly does make one heck of a pina colada.

The Voice of Sneffle the Baker, who lives in the Dragon's Throat, is played by Val Bettin, who has too many voice over credits to list, but who recently played the Sultan of Agraba (Aladdin) for Disney. Val Bettin is also the voice of Sneffle the Baker on the Dungeon Master's answering machine, and the voice of the Flickering Torch.

THE WIZARD BELBOZ

Belboz appears only briefly in Zork Grand Inquisitor, to instruct the player about the nature of the treasures that must be reclaimed to restore magic to the Empire.

Phillipe Clarke plays the voice of the Wizard Belboz, as well as the voice of the Inquisition Propaganda Dioramas.

> *Note:* *There are a whole host of other voices and voice actors in the game—ranging from a Spell Checker to the curfew-bound inhabitants of Foozle, to a telephone operator in Hell. Just play the game already.*

Chapter III:
The Backstory

*...OR, HOW THE MAGIC WARS CAME TO BE:
THE DEEP BACKSTORY OF ZORK GRAND INQUISITOR IN WHICH CERTAIN THINGS ARE REASONABLY EXPLAINED AND A GREAT MANY OTHERS ARE QUITE UNREASONABLY NOT.*

WITH REGARD TO LUCKLESS ADVENTURERS

This is the tale of how Magic was banished from the Empire, and how a luckless adventurer, looking for nothing except a few zorkmids and a bit of treasure, stumbled across a seemingly useless brass lamp, and into a bit more than he had bargained for—the Magic Underground.

LONG, LONG AGO— THE LAST GOLDEN AGE OF MAGIC

What is Magic? Is it a business? Is it a philosophy? A religion? A source of power or equilibrium? Is it to be disturbed or balanced? These are precisely the sort of naïve questions that two novice first-years debated at GUE Tech, Zork's famed Magic University. The good-natured, chubby Dalboz of Gurth, and the sharp-eyed, sharp-tongued Mir Yannick, were unlikely roommates. Dalboz, who was by all accounts the talent of the two, found himself drawn to the University for a variety of inexplicable reasons, and one quite explicable one: He scored so high on the entrance exam, he not only had The Gift, but in fact qualified as Highly Gifted, and could attend free of charge on a Vice Regent's Scholarship. The Trustees were dumbfounded; how could the son of a simple Miner from Gurth possess such Natural Magic? The Miner himself was dismissive of the whole affair, and warned his son of involving himself in the useless chicanery of enchantment. The Miner himself was, as you say, disenchanted.

THE ODDEST OF
ODD DUCKS

Truthfully, Dalboz was an odd duck, if pleasant; there was an indisputable muchness to his character, an overflowing of his person and nature and, indeed, everything he came in contact with seemed to spring to life. He heard a great clamour of voices where there was none. He was always hungry, and had never, to his knowledge, felt what it was like to be full. And if he were to simply drop a seed in a garden, a full plant would spring up and bear fruit within a manner of seconds. If you looked closely enough, the story goes, you could see grass spring up in his footsteps as he walked down the street. He was a Natural Mage, of a very simple—if crude—nature. (But what is the power of nature, if not simple and crude?) Had he been born in another time, he would have been as great as Megaboz, though a good deal less agitated.

MERELY ANOTHER
YANNICK

Mir Yannick did not have the Gift, but he and Dalboz grew to be friends, all the same. It is commonly held that those who cannot practice Magic cannot understand the practice of Magic, either; whether or not this is so, it is true that Mir seemed a bit literal in his interpretation of the Higher Lessonry of Thaumaturgy—a bit forced of Hand in Basic Enchanting—and certainly, his sneering, bottom-line orientation towards the whole Business of Magic did not win him any favors with the faculty.

But... if you take into consideration that Mir's father, a yeoman farmer who bred platypus for pie, was paying 500 zm a term so that his son could learn the proper spell set to make his grain grow golden and tall (the "THROCK" spell, causing plants to grow) and his platypi grow fat and furry (a variant of the "CONBAK" spell, causing bodies to grow in twelve ways) so that at the end of the year the "profits" ledger might for once equal the "costs"—you, too, might come to evaluate Magic in terms of its affordability, profitability, and fiduciary viability. Mir himself was named when his expectant mother told his father, Yannick the Elder, that she had a surprise for him, and he had to guess what it was. He guessed a sack of gold, a sack of wheat, and finally even a good, sturdy sack. So when his wife answered him, "Nay, merely another Yannick," Mir Yannick found the unfortunate name had stuck. One can imagine Mir's own expectations of his life were somewhat as low.

A DECIDING VOTE

And in truth, athough many Enchanters in the GUE have no natural inclination towards the subject, and would have just as soon been barristers or barkeepers—were there openings available at these more popular guilds—there are some who are altogether immagical. Try as he may, at the end of his first year exams, Mir could no more make a field grow than he could make a platypus fatten. In fact, everything he touched seemed to wither and die. His grades continued to falter, and the same week Dalboz made the Mage's List, Mir was put on probation. When the Trustees were called to approve Dalboz's qualifications for the appointment to Mage, they stayed after to vote on Mir's expulsion. Mir made it by one vote—and if Dalboz were not so good at the "ZEMDOR" Spell (turn things into triplicate), he would have been out by two.

THE DAM FIGHT

Mir never fully realized what Dalboz had conjured up on his behalf, to cheat the vote and keep him enrolled at GUE Tech. Instead—and you may think this somewhat ironic, unless you too have had an overachieving friend—he recruited a group of popular upper-classmen Conjurers (bullies, really) to confront Dalboz, and have some fun at his expense. When they tried to stop him on his way to class, Dalboz fled to the Underground Subway. Mir and his bullies chased him from car to car as he tried in vain to get away. When Dalboz saw the train stop at the famed Flood Control Dam #3, he leapt off the train and headed for the top of the Dam.

Perhaps he thought that tossing a few "VAXUM" spells (make a hostile creature your friend) behind him would end the matter. Perhaps the slightly flabby freshman was too out of breath to think clearly. In either case, once Dalboz reached the edge of the Dam, he soon found himself surrounded. Mir accused Dalboz of having cast a "NUMDUM" spell upon him. (A Numdum spell is a common stupidity spell that lesser enchanters particularly liked to cast upon one another, as a kind of hazing prank at GUE institutions.) Despite Dalboz's proclamations of loyalty, Mir invoked—well, Mir attempted to invoke, but after turning purple and spluttering to such an extent that the Conjurers took over for him—a "KULKAD" spell in return. (A Kulkad spell, of course, is the spell that will dispel spells.)

However, since the only spell in operation was the "ZEMDOR" spell that had kept Mir from being expelled, a Certificate of Expulsion instantly appeared in Mir's hands. The upperclassmen began to laugh, and Mir, furious with rage and embarrassment, tore the certificate in half and—before anyone could stop him—pitched Dalboz over the side of Flood Control Dam #3.

But Dalboz held fast to Mir's cloak, and when he flopped over the side, he took his roommate with him. All who witnessed the event were certain the friends were plunging to their deaths. As the two friends went screaming towards the bottom far below, Dalboz—in possibly the most important invocation in his career—cast a long-life spell upon himself and his roommate, and the two bounced up from the rock, as if made of soft Borphean rubber.

A PEACE IS MADE

Mir was quite ashamed of himself, and Dalboz, to his credit, was equally forgiving. He did everything he could to mend their friendship, which ultimately included expelling everyone in the entire school, to negate the expulsion and, in fact, make it somewhat of a promotion, seeing that Mir was actually the first to be expelled at all. Mir never apologized, but Dalboz knew that to bear the shame of a public encounter with one's own, honest stupidity, was far worse than any apology he could require. What Dalboz couldn't have known was the depth of the hatred Mir felt, not just for Dalboz, but for Magic itself and the shame and self-loathing it brought him. What Dalboz never saw was the sight of

Mir, night after night, slipping into the the archive of GUE Tech, burning precious scrolls of High Magic, a few at a time. That much less to learn; that much less shame. Mir Yannick vowed to destroy Magic—and Dalboz with it—before it ruined him.

Yet, in their own awkward fashion, the two schoolmates remained cordial. Possibly this is because neither Mir nor Dalboz were the run of the mill, ale-swilling, mage-bonding sort of student enchanter that had any friends at all. And Mir always needed Dalboz's help in order to pass his exams. In return, Mir would ply Dalboz with platypus pot pies, sent in a picnic basket from home. In fact, the only bit of cruelty Mir ever showed Dalboz after the incident at the Space Needle, was an endless needling about his girth ("Well, they don't call you Dalboz of Gurth for nothing!")—about which Dalboz became a bit sensitive, especially considering Mir's athletic, farm-bred physique.

THE THIRD DUNGEON MASTER

But friends of a fashion they were; and in 966, when the Second Dungeon Master (whose True Name is known only by the Master of Naming, who is, handily enough, the Second Dungeon Master himself) appeared to Dalboz, and bequeathed to him the Dungeon Master's Staff—saying only that Destiny had appointed the prodigy Dalboz the Third Dungeon Master of the empire—Mir was the first person to congratulate him, if not warmly.

In fact, Mir was the only person to congratulate him at all, because only moments after Dalboz became the Third, word arrived from Borphee that the University was closing immediately. There had been an accident, a mishandling of Magic, and a powerful mage had knocked the Cosmic Equilibrium out of balance—destroying the entire Age of Magic in the name of his improving his own power. Small wonder the Second DM was so hasty about dumping that staff and beating a quick retreat; Dalboz was fated to become, it seemed, the only DM to never hold office. And though the Staff made a lovely walking stick, and apparently there was some sort of housing associated with the position, Dalboz fell into a wretched state of despair.

Mir, of course, enjoyed this turn of events immensely. Though he tried to console Dalboz with the rumor around school—that all Magic had been crammed into the Coconut of Quendor, where it would be watched over, until the return of Magic itself—he secretly scoffed at the notion. But, as the roommates parted ways that evening, at the Crossroads of the Great Underground Highway, they pledged to meet again, should that great day ever come. Their lives were woven together in the Long Life Spell; they would certainly meet each other again, under happier circumstances. Or so they thought at the time.

And with that, they dragged their bags in separate directions down the Great Underground Highway.

THE NEXT CENTURY— A MAGICAL HIATUS

Dalboz retired to a cottage in the Underground—truly the only perk of the office of Dungeon Master, when you consider the Dungeon Master is responsible for magically paying his own pension via the Quelbo Spell (Turns Ripe Coconuts into Gold.) Without Magic, coconuts were just coconuts, and Dalboz was broke, horribly depressed, and quite bored. Not to mention, utterly lacking in appetite. As a recluse, he became a Thaumaturge, a Philosopher of Theories Magicall & Hypotheticall. Excepting a seven year period in which he did absolutely nothing at all except play Single Fanucci (the Solitary Version) and drink Accardian Ale, he spent a good 35 years working out the answer to the freshman conundrum posed by the Bozbar Spell: "If you cause an animal to sprout wings somewhere in the Universe, somewhere else in the Universe, does another animal lose its wings?" (The answer being, "Yes.") Depressed and alone, he devoted the next 70 years to studies of a more pressing issue; that being, could a fundamentally Magic Land be suppressed of Magic, forever?

DEVOTION OF OTHER SORTS

While the Third Dungeon Master faded into obscurity, Mir, meanwhile, did the only thing the untitled second-son of a yeoman farmer could do in an age without Magic—he joined a Zorkastrian Seminary. Though he would be of no use in the platypus-fattening department, perhaps he could at least pray for the financial security of his family, Mir's father reasoned. And so it seemed Mir had finally found the perfect calling for a slightly lazy, fairly greedy, and moderately-educated person with no particular skills of any sort— he became a Zorkastrian Brother. Master Mir was spectacularly relieved to not have to know much, be able to do much, or even be in possession of some sort of predetermined Destiny. He just kept his mouth shut, kissed a few rings, and mumbled something while he stared intently into the Fires. Magic? He didn't have to know Magic; it was forbidden! His Brothers despised the Magical Arts—and praise Yoruk for that!

Mir found that by bartering with his superiors over student directories of True Names, stolen from the admissions office (not Call Names, as you or I might refer to each other, but the True Names—of High Magic—that are the source of one's personal power), Mir might accomplish the double purpose of avenging himself on all those who ever laughed at him, and ingratiating himself with Zorkastrian officials. It worked better than Mir ever hoped; his classmates found themselves under perpetual surveilliance, as infidels and heretics, and Mir himself quickly became Master Mir, Father Mir, Elder Mir, and then Bishop Mir. By the time the reclusive Dalboz had formulated the answer to his Bozbar Postulate, Mir had ascended to the calling of First Archbishop in High Office of the Grand Inquisitor of Zork. And he no longer had time to return Dalboz's rambling, boring, letters, filled with useless packets of rare and newly cultivated Seeds, which the Archbishop promptly threw into the fire. Mir was no longer interested in talk of Magic. He was interested in Power. And he was interested in something more than talk.

WHITE COLLAR CRIME

Mir understood that if Magic was, indeed, finally going away, in its departure lay a real opportunity to persecute those who had once enjoyed such Magic Power. Mir could finally wreak his revenge on all who had ever practiced the thaumaturgical arts; he would not be satisfied until he saw to it that his one-time classmates (the same Conjurer Bullies who had laughed at the Numdum incident) were confined in the dark recesses of the Steppinthrax Dungeon. The Grand Inquisitor would not listen to Mir—who was calling for a good old-fashioned inquisition. Mir was disgusted; if he were the Grand Inquisitor, he would champion the death of Magic...

CHIEF UNDERSECRETARY WARTLE

It wasn't until Mir heard the confession of convicted criminal embezzler Undersecretary Wartle, the Undersecretary to the Undersecretary to the Secretary of the Zork Patents Office, during the Archbishop's sojourn in the Wonderfully Horrid White-Collar Confessions Ministry, that he knew how his Destiny should unfold. After handing out a number of Hail Yoruks, Mir opened the confessional and offered an alternate rehabilitative plan: He would use his influence with the Grand Inquisitor to demand a full pardon from Syovar III, if Wartle would begin altering a few patents for unique Zork technologies, here and there, transferring them into Mir's possession, as only a partially reformed patents embezzler knew how. Mir became certain that his rise to power and fortune—not to mention his vengeance upon Magic—would lie with technology. Though popular sentiment had long held that technology was for stupid people (in a word, Numdums)—inferior people who had no Magic to them—in the new, anti-magicall economy, technology would become invaluable. A new Magic, belonging exclusively to Archbishop Mir himself.

Wartle, who always had been spineless, fell under the spell of the Archbishop's ambition immediately (whoever said Mir had no Magic to him?)—and by the time Mir had succeeded to the High Office of Grand Inquisitor himself (and while still sorrowing over the unfortunate demise of the previous Grand Inquisitor, who seemed to have eaten a rather lethally rancid platypus pot pie) he possessed the patent to every known piece of registered, trademarked, and patented technology in the Great Underground Empire. He even went so far as to resurrect the famed, abandoned Frobozz Magic Company—as the Frobozz Electric Company. And in this manner, the seeds of the Inquisition fell from his barren hand...

MAGIC SEEDS ITS SLOW RETURN

Back in the cottage of the Dungeon Master, the Master himself dangled from a noose until he was purple and bruised from the rope. But it was no use. Sighing, he cut himself free—and stabbed the dagger repeatedly into his chest, with all the inattention of a bored child. Not even a drop of blood appeared on the blade. How desperately he wished he had never cast that Long Life Spell; for he would kill himself a thousand times, before he could bare another day of the monotony of a life without Magic. His house was cluttered with Fanucci Pieces from a final, solitary game of 3-D Single Fanucci that he had been playing for several years now; and as a result, he could barely walk through his kitchen, without knocking over the markers of his Fanucci Hand—a Lobster and a Snail. Ears and Lamps were littered across the table top—and Bugs, Plungers, and Inkblots lay in every other square of the black and white parquet of his kitchen floor.

Just as the Dungeon Master was dragging a large sack of non-magical, combustible gun powder out to the garden, in hopes of exploding himself in the garden tool shed, he stopped dead in his tracks (no pun intended). He dropped to the garden ground, and stared in disbelief as a Magicall Seedling pushed its way through the soil, blooming into the strangest, most fabulous looking flower ever seen in a matter of seconds. A moment later, and the DM's Magic Flower and Vegetable Garden had sprung into life, bursting into all sorts of egg plants and auto plants and office plants and parts plants and trans-plants once again. The DM was exultant; his second postulate, the oft-disparaged "Treatise on the Insuppressability of Magic in a Fundamentally Magic Land" had been correct after all. The GUE would, eventually, begin to right itself. The Balance of Things Magicall and Otherwise could not be held, unreckoned, for eternity. The time had finally come for Magic to begin its slow return to Zork.

Dalboz determined to pay a visit to his long-lost friend, the Grand Inquisitor. They had not spoken in many years now, but Dalboz knew they still shared the bond of the Long-Life Spell. In its weaving, he had linked their Destinies, and their paths must yet be resolved. Maybe things would go better between them, he reasoned, now that Magic was on its way back to the Empire. But first, a bit of supper... and he snipped a couple of hard-boiled eggs off the vine.

THE TOTEMIZER IS DISCOVER'D

The Grand Inquisitor listened with impatience as Wartle read him "The Signs of the Times" (Section B of the *New Zork Times*). There were unmistakable signs throughout the Empire: Magic creatures awakening, Magic Spell Scrolls materializing, a few Enchanters regaining limited powers. The Grand Inquisitor was gloomy; for his Frobozz Electric Company, the Return of Magic promised nothing but a loss of power and capital. Without Magic, the Inquisitor governed a monopoly of industries that made him a higher power than any one religion could. He had nothing to gain from even Vice Regent Syovar III, who had grown particularly troublesome as of late, just as the GI was reaching the height of his power. They had been arguing over what change in policy need be driven by the alleged return of Magic. At first, Syovar III had been in favor of Mir's pro-posed (and rather extreme) Inquisition, believing the GI when he preached Magic as the harbinger of social anarchy and political unrest. He had not complained when the Anti-Magic Propaganda had gone up, nor when the Propaganda P.A. System had been installed. Yet, when the GI had begun the Magic Trials, the Vice Regent had grown suddenly strangely populist. Syovar was siding with his people, over the Council of Generals. The GI had no other recourse but to meet with the Council—privately. And a difficult decision had been made.

Truly, the GI could not have hoped for more terrible timing for the whispering, insidious, reappearance of Magic. He was now only days from asserting the final phase of his rise to power—the Council Approved Removal of the Vice Regent himself. And even if the removal of the Regent were successful, what was to be done with the reappearing Magic? Magic, unlike mere human flesh, cannot be destroyed simply because its use-creature is "killed." Magic, like some strangely radioactive Thaddeum waste, must be contained. Like a reverberating vibration along a wire, Magic resonates ten-fold once freed of physical form. All that binds a magicall property to its physical form is how it is Named, by way of the Old Speech, the ancient, magicall language of the Empire, the language that lends its runic power to every woven spell. Somehow, magicall creatures must be Un-Named. If Nameless, then powerless.

But how to accomplish the Un-Naming? Surely this problem had been encountered previously, in the long history of the Empire. Was there any technology, any industry in his control that could be revamped, readjusted a bit, to provide some kind of containment to the rise of Magic in the Empire? Hastily, with fear of displeasing his master, Wartle searched out a handful of out-of-date patents—including one for a massive, misshapen machine, a remnant from the Flathead Dynasty—when Enchanters were plenty and plenty troublesome, and Lord Dimwit was always looking for some way to control them. Perhaps it would prove to be just the thing.

Twice, an Assassination

At first, the DM had tried to just teleport to the Steppinthrax Monastary Headquarters of the GI. But he could get only the most part of his left foot to prematurely disappear; there was still insufficient Magic in the atmosphere. He begrudgingly settled for riding a lumbering Hungus, which he absolutely detested, partly because it was slow and uncomfortable when one knew one had the option of instantaneous travel, and also because he never knew exactly what to do with his hands. Dungeon Masters, like most Wizards, are terrible at accomplishing everyday, menial tasks, without the use of Magic. This DM was no exception to the rule; there was at least enough Magic for the reins to hold themselves, so the DM could carry with him the rapidly growing Hard-Boiled Eggplant; a token of friendship for his skeptical friend. Magic had begun its slow reassertion. Of that, the DM was certain.

A BLOODY REUNION

When the DM finally reached the Steppinthrax Monastary Headquarters and Museum, he was told the Grand Inquisitor could not be disturbed. He waited in the lobby for quite some time. Just as he was staring up at the massive propaganda posters of his old schoolmate, and wondering at what strange goings-on he had missed while in his deep seclusion, he heard anguished screams from the GI's office—the sounds of a violent struggle. The DM tried to dematerialize, and then, giving up, fumbled with the door for some time, before he remembered about the knob, and pushed inside...

THE HEAD OF STATE DIVIDED

...Only to find the GI himself standing over the slain body of Syovar, whose head was neatly cleft in twain, and lying in a growing puddle of blood. As the GI explained, Wartle had retrieved several useful technologies dating back to Dimwit Flathead, the least of these being this deceptively simple iron cap, known to the enemies of the Flathead Dynasty as the "Maidenhead." TheMaidenhead employed the traditionally lethal technique of the Iron Maiden, to the head of the victim only, so that the effect became one of instant Flat-headedness. And of course, death.

The Dungeon Master seemed strangely steeled by the discovery, as if some part of him had been waiting for the GI to reveal his true colors for a very long time. Then, circling the body, the two old friends began to argue bitterly over the ramifications of both the assassination and the return of Magic. The Dungeon Master argued that Zork was an enchanted land, that could not be ruled except by Magic, or by its consent. The Grand Inquisitor knew, however, that he himself could not rule—as per his designs—if Magic were allowed back into the Empire... he would be impotent next to the reunited, reinvigorated Enchanters' Guild. He begged the DM to help him put down Magic, and reclaim the Empire. The DM refused. He looked down at the magicall plant in his hands—and it curled into itself, instantly withering into a dead stalk. The DM looked up at his old friend sadly, suddenly understanding what was about to happen. He turned to go, disgusted. He said only two words. "Tell them."

Then, the GI sprung open the Maidenhead, which clamped itself to the DM—just as his clothes fell to the ground, empty. Though he first appeared dead—his body had, after all, disappeared in a cloud of gray smoke—the GI was left to suspect that he had pronounced some kind of protective spell on himself, the moment before he was struck.

He didn't notice a small brass lantern, of the typical Adventurer's style, rocking slightly on the floor by the slain Regent. Had he seen it, he might have saved himself a considerable heap of trouble.

LUCY FLATHEAD: A WITNESS TO THE CRIME

Lucy stared, transfixed, at the slain Vice Regent's photo in the *New Zork Times* that lay on her desk at the Port Foozle Psychic Friends Bureau, beneath the headline, "Syovar Assasinated; Who Will Succeed?" She was getting a migraine, an awful migraine. She tried even harder to ignore the picture that was taking shape in her mind. It had something to do with the death of the Regent—but it hurt too much to see it. And she didn't particularly care for whatever it was. She was not, by nature, a political person. She believed that people were weak and foolish; that horrible things either had or would befall them; that fate was cruel and purposeless. She knew the first of these precepts best illustrated by her own frivolous ancestry; the second from glimpsing into the grim minds of her clientele; and the last, from her own dark life. So what did she care if one more fat politician got his due?

She turned her attention to the distractingly lewd observances blaring out from the mind of the customer that sat across from her. His was the most dismal sort, a petty gambler looking to hedge his odds in the windcat races. It was precisely this sort of client that made her wonder if her Gift were actually a Gift at all. This was her fourth job as a Psychic Counselor; in an age devoid of Magic, a whole market for bogus psychic carpet-baggers had sprung up in its place. She had never let on to the others at the Bureau that she was an actual Telepath, partly out of a kind of professional courtesy—because they were scalawags and scams and she did not want to them to feel badly that she was not—and partly because she was embarrassed. And once people knew she knew what they were thinking, they became rather embarrassed, themselves. Especially the men.

With her telepathic abilities came a checkered lineage of which she was publicly quite defensive—and privately, quite ashamed. Though she wore an ill-fitting headpiece to try to hide it, Lucy's head was absolutely flat; she was one of the last surviving descendants of the House of Flathead. Her extended family had been forced into hiding long ago, with the fall of the Flathead Empire. Her own ancestors had lived in the catacombs beneath the prison where her namesake, Lucrezia Flathead, had been secretly executed two hundred years ago. Apparently Lucrezia had given birth to a child while she was in captivity—sired by a powerful Enchanter who was imprisoned for refusing to attend Dimwit's ridiculous Coronation. Though he could have easily freed himself from any prison, he fell madly in love with Lucrezia, a much-maligned—and quite wrongly so, Lucy would argue, from a revisionist, feminist perspective on the matter—free spirit of a most singular nature. Yet Lucrezia had angered her own people, and the House of Flathead was not, by nature, forgiving. Not even an Enchanter could protect Lucrezia from the hired guns charged with dispatching the Murderess ("Divorcee," Lucy would correct) to the Great Beneath.

When Lucrezia met her final misfortune, the Enchanter spirited the child away to the recesses of the deepest underground, known only as The Dark. It took all he could do to protect the child from the terrible Curse on the House of Flathead—and only when he was certain that the child was to be spared, the Enchanter disappeared, completely sapped of his powers. He was last seen in the general direction of Miznia, near Gurth. Rumor had it he had fallen to work as a lowly Miner... perhaps started another family... but he had never been heard of again.

In the years to follow, the women descendants of this remarkable child were still protected from the Curse, and continued to be born with the traditionally flat heads, which they tried to hide, still fearing for their lives. They remained in The Dark, apart from the rest of the Empire. Flat heads aside, in every generation there appeared to be one daughter such as Lucy, who, quite obviously, was a telepath.

Yet for one gifted in the reading of minds, Lucy had no such skill with the reading of hearts. Like all of the descendants of Lucrezia before her, Lucy had inherited her general mistrust of all men. Lucy was cold, dismissive of emotions, generally, because they tended to cloud her readings of minds—like static, or poor reception on a telephone line. She was dismissive of emotions, personally, because she had never had any of the nicer varieties. The Dark was not, ultimately, a wonderful place to raise a child.

When the pain became so unbearable that she could no longer listen to the blather in the customer's head, Lucy had no choice but to let it out. She threw back her head—surprising the customer—and allowed the strange, violet light to flow out of her eyes, flooding the room. Her co-workers stared at her with amazement, as her seemingly lifeless form floated a few feet above the ground. In her trance, Lucy saw in a few harsh stills the death of Syovar—and at the hand of the Grand Inquisitor. She saw the death of the Dungeon Master, as well, and startled when she saw him—even now, from the grave—look her in the eye, imploring "Tell them." And with that, Lucy fell to the ground.

She had no choice. The Dungeon Master had sent her the vision, and she had to do something because of it. Lucy left the Bureau immediately, never to return. She made her way to the Magistrate, and took her own deposition, sealing it in a file at the Magistrate's Office. She gave it to the Magistrate, and panicking, got out of town.

Lucy had made it to the shore, and was waiting to board the Ferry to Accardia, when the Grand Inquisitor's men found her and bound her over to trial for High Treason Against the Empire. The Magistrate had broken the seal on her file, and alerted the GI immediately. Implicating the GI—the only remaining authority that held the temporary government of the Empire together, in the time of flux and chaos following the death of the Vice Regent—rapidly earned Lucy a sentence of Death. The fact that the Grand Inquisitor was the presiding official of the court did not help matters much, but it did somewhat speed up the deliberations. Though she fully expected to die, the Grand Inquisitor had other plans for her.

THE MAGIC INQUISITION

The Grand Inquisitor had appointed Undersecretary Wartle, and a certain number of trustworthy men, to the task of Magic Surveillance. Soon after the death of the Dungeon Master, reports began to flood in. The land appeared to be quickened and invigorated, growing with Magicall Life again; just as in the DM's garden, enchanted trees sprang from seeds, some bearing ripe, splitting fruit in a single moment; others producing umbrellas or thermoses or galoshes and other such sundry items. Along the Highway, a Magicall Sword of Elvish Workmanship sprouted up from the land in a strange, sealed box. And someone had even reported strange activities at the deserted university. The Grand Inquisitor knew he had to get things under control, and he hadn't very long. Magic was on the Rise; his propaganda campaign seemed not to be stopping it, but instead sending it Underground. People were starting to hope.

Wartle had, in fact, produced not only the patents, but the very machines first employed by Dimwit Flathead for the same hostile purpose—controlling the magicall masses. When Lucy Flathead was sentenced to Death, therefore, the Grand Inquisitor enjoyed not only the pleasurable surge of power that lay in giving her the sentence, (for he really was a very horrid man, as these things go) but yet another in commuting it. Now that he had the attention of the population, he determined to make an example of Lucy, and brought her to the Totemizer, a strange machine her people had invented so long ago.

Though she would not give him the satisfaction of showing her fear, the Totemizer was truly a hideous machine, like a giant meat grinder, with spikes and spokes and five bloits of copper tubing, wrapped around and around and around. Though the effect of this monstrous device was not lethal, it was forcibly anti-magical; that is, only this device could physically accomplish the Un-Naming, by separating magicall essence from physical matter—rendering Nameless, and thus Useless, the given magic of any Being. Lucy, who was born into Middle Magic, and given her True Name through the power of the Old Speech upon the third day following her birth, would lose her visionary powers when she lost her Name. She would become captive in a disc of base metal without substance, a lifeless totem of her Magicall self.

In the final moments that Lucy stood atop this giant mechanical spectacle, she became something of a folk hero to the crowd at its base. The Grand Inquisitor, who was more taken with the vision of her body than her visionary mind, offered her a last chance at clemency if she were to subject herself to an inquisition of a more personal nature. To this she only spat out "Murderer."

Then, her eyes began to radiate the same strange purple light—and up she floated, straining against the ropes that bound her to the platform of the machine. She began to speak in a low monotone, warning the Grand Inquisitor of his doom in a strange vision. There would be only one, one who would call the Great Lady down from the Planes of Atrii, through the Last Door. She would come for Mir, and only a great sacrifice and a brave heart would destroy him.

The frightened Grand Inquisitor could bear no more of such nonsense, and slapped her... hard. In whipping her head to the side, her hair seemed to move, and then the top of her headdress sailed cleanly off—revealing her truer, flatter nature. The crowd hushed, shocked. Lucy was a Flathead! There were still Flatheads living in the Empire? How could this be?

But Lucy, now herself, just smiled defiantly. When her ropes were loosened, she laughed at the Grand Inquisitor, and threw herself into the machine.

CHAPTER III: THE BACKSTORY

ANTHARIA JACK

A passing mercenary stared at her, transfixed. Antharia Jack—for that was his name, as he was known among fellow Adventurers—fought his way to the front of the crowd, desperate for one last glimpse. But a small explosion sent him reeling back, followed by a great whirl, then sparks and smoke, and you could just make out where something passed through the tubes, spiraling downward, around and around. An iron totem fell to the stone floor with a clatter. Lucy was no more.

THE GRIFF: A VICTIM OF THE INQUISITION

As the Grand Inquisitor tightened his control on the land, he coaxed the Council of the Generals—a tribunal of war heroes that controlled various political and tribal factions throughout the Empire—into an alliance based on their shared exploitation of the people and resources of the Empire. As the GI's power expanded, he began to train the GUE population increasingly towards technology, and away from Magic. The GI owned, and thus could control, all of the existing technology in the Empire—and with it, the people. Magic was unruly and uncontrollable, and the GI made it quite clear that no type of Magic, of any purpose, was tolerable in the Empire. Anything that even smelled of the return of enchantment was to be shunned, and ultimately, destroyed.

The Inquisition proved most unfortunate for the many races of Magic, Halfling-Magic, or Barely Magic Creatures that lived in Zork. Inquisition troops, known as The Inquisition Riders, canvassed the land, hunting down Trolls, Orcs, Nymphs, Sprites, and so forth. One day, when a lone member of the Guard patrolled a singularly dense forest glade, he came across a winged, tailed creature—like a soft, cuddly dragon—thrashing in a trap they had set the week before. His tail was caught by a rope, which was tied to a stake in the ground, and prevented him from flying away, no matter how hard he strained at it.

As the Guard pulled at his rope, the creature began to hiss and grimace, as if he were trying to breathe fire from his little feline jaws. The soldier burst into laughter, and began to taunt the fellow in a most unfortunate manner.

At that point, the Griff—for he was exactly that—began to babble in the most idiotic fashion. He was trying to speak in the Old Speech, the ancient runic language that empowers Dragons above all other Magicall creatures. Of course, he didn't actually know Old Speech, which hampered the effort considerably, and he wasn't a Dragon, which pretty much finished the job. Then, he began to shout—"Avert your eyes! Look away! I'm a Dragon, you know. If you dare look into my eyes, I will turn you to... to... jelly." The shouting became stammering, because frankly, there isn't anything too frightening about jelly, even if one wouldn't want to be it oneself, and actually, everyone knows that looking into a Dragon's eyes will turn you not to jelly but to stone. The Guard came closer, grabbing the Griff by the chin and staring into his eyes. "It's stone, you idiot. Not Jelly."

The Griff, who was by nature quite timid and could not bare to be touched in anything he interpreted to be a rough fashion, shrieked and cowered to the far extreme of the length of rope, flapping his wings as hard as he could, and begging—above all—not to be hurt. He wasn't a bad fellow, really, he was just a simple coward, a bit of tragedian, and touch neurotic about anything potentially involving pain of any sort. And if he did seem to imagine that nobody liked him, that everyone talked about him the second he hopped—er, flew—out of the room, and that he was the butt of every joke, you must take a moment to consider how it must feel to be compared every moment to a Dragon, and to always suffer by the comparison. The Griff was not so fearsome, so loathsome, and, in a terrible kind of a way, so handsome, as a real Dragon—he could not smash things with his tail, had no protective Dragon scales or powerful Dragon breath, and his belly was not armored in golden treasure. In fact, he only very rarely had any treasure at all.

But he did have a treasure, once. His magical race had once been protected by a Magicall talisman—the Coconut of Quendor—that they had stumbled upon, quite by chance, aboard a haunted ship in the Great Seas long ago. Bound in a powerful incantation by the enchanter Y'Gael, the Coconut was the spellbound keeper of a desperate purpose—the preservation of all Magic ever known to the Empire. Whoever had the Coconut in their protection was fulfilling a Magicall destiny, and could not be harmed. For many years, the Griffs flourished as they carefully hoarded the Coconut. Then a greedy hoard of Dragons fell upon them, and the Coconut was lost to the Empire, last seen in the talons of a great, flying Dragon—somewhere in the vicinity of the Great Seas.

All that remained was a bedtime tale told to Griff pups, of a sinister Dragon Archipelago, filled with the Rolling Isles, that rose and sank above and below the water, bobbing like a buoy in the waves. On one of those islands lived the fiercest Dragon of all, the Old Watchdragon, guardian of the Coconut for the past hundred years. Only the bravest, most important Griff in the world would defeat the Old Watchdragon, and reclaim the Coconut for his race. Or so the story went. Without the Coconut, the Griffs were quite defenseless—lacking the natural protection of their armored Dragon cousins—and had dwindled in number to the point where there were only a handful left in the entire Empire.

This particular Griff had never been in a battle, or for that matter, even a fight—and he was petrified by the idea of fighting this Guard, now. It was only a matter of minutes before he was reduced to a blubbering pup, and only a matter of days before he stood at the top of the Totemizer Machine, begging for clemency. But a Magic Race is a Magic Race, and there was no room for Magic of any sorts in the Grand Inquisitor's new regime. The troops had been teasing the Griff for some time, provoking him until he began to sob with such vigor that even Grand Inquisitor began to feel a bit uncomfortable. Just as the GI gave the signal for the Griff to be pushed into the machine...

✝ THE BROGMOID

...A squat, hairy creature—a Brogmoid Guard, who had felt badly for the Griff, and shown him many preferences while in jail—leaped up out of the crowd and, ripping a massive iron tube off the side of the Totemizer, knocked a Guard down into the machine instead of the Griff. And, for one tense moment, the Grand Inquisitor himself wobbled on the edge of the Totemizer; he would have fallen inside, if he hadn't caught the Guard with his hands, and knocked him into the machine by way of keeping himself from falling. Chaos ensued, and when the chase was over and done, it took six men (each twice the size of a Brog) to hold down the wrathful, growling Brogmoid, while a seventh stuffed the Griff down the hatch.

A whirr… and smoke… and sparks… and a metal totem clattered to the stone floor. A Rider picked it up and bit it, as if checking to see if it were a real coin. He rode away with it, down the Great Highway, but he never knew what became of it after that. Perhaps it fell through a hole in his pocket.

A HERO BECOMES A VICTIM

As you can imagine, the Brogmoid made a quick visit, the next day, to the court. Brogmoids had all the characteristics of the creatures born into the Deep Magic of the Underground; though they knew little of spells, and less of everything else, Brogmoids possessed an unsurpassable strength, and an insupressable temper to match it. The short, stout hotheads had been known to flatten men twice their size, over a chance comment misinterpreted as an insult to their honor. When their extreme stupidity was at its dullest, even the slightest "Excuse me" could result in a breathtaking squeeze from an obliging Brog. But with such thick wits come brave hearts; and indeed, those who know nothing, fear nothing. In this regard, the Brog and the Griff could not have been more unlike.

But luckily, or almost luckily, for the Griff, this Brog, in particular, possessed a singular, if instinctual, compassion that made it physically impossible for him to sit and watch while a harmless and defenseless creature like the Griff was tormented for pleasure. This big-hearted Brog was one of the nicest fellows a Griff could ever hope to meet; in fact, there was no creature, great or small, that would refuse to converse with him, no matter how dull the conversation would invariably be. This Brog was forever in trouble as an Inquisition Guard, seeing as his locker was full of all sorts of forbidden things the prisoners would implore him to bring them. Not much harm it could do in there, he reasoned—if you could call it that—though he personally didn't see what was so appetizing about a honeycake with a metal file or skeleton key stuck in the middle. When he tried them, they got terribly stuck in his teeth. But if someone needed something, however much their tastes differed from his, he would do it for them. He was just that sort of a fellow.

hat didn't make much of a defense in his speedy trial in the Court of the Inquisition, but the Brog didn't really understand much of what was said in there to begin with. When asked "How do you plead?" the Brog looked at the Magistrate like he was stupid, and said "Like this." Then he got down on his hands and knees and said "Please, Please, oh I beg you." If you can imagine the rest of the trial along those same lines, you won't be far off.

When he was finally taken to the Totemizer machine, it was in a massive metal collar, and two sets of chains. Twenty guards hoisted him up to the top of the machine, and the Grand Inquisitor wasted not a minute dawdling, this time around.

A whirr... and smoke... and sparks... and a metal totem clattered to the stone floor.

GREATER PORT FOOZLE: ANTHARIA JACK'S PAWN SHACK

Poor Jack's romance with Lucy (albeit a bit one-sided, considering that only Jack saw her and they actually never spoke), was just another chapter in the bumpy road of stardom and menial clerkships that Jack had traversed.

Born to stalk Adventuring folk that tended to live far too long, Jack was the worst Adventurer there is—afraid of the dark, unable to draw a map, and terrible at carrying items, even in a sack.

So, with his parents shamed by their son's inability to quest, Jack enrolled at the Antharia School of Drama. By sheer luck he landed a part in the Z-Team when he stumbled onto stage during open rehearsals. (And when we say stumbled, we mean, in the sense of, fell on his face.) It turns out that the Executive Producer of the show, Syovar I, was looking for someone to take a pie in the face at least once an episode. Jack was it.

Jack took his money and opened a Casino in Port Foozle, content to retirement after the show was canceled. But fate won't leave you alone if you are on its list for greater tidbits of immortality.

In less than a week, Jack won the Cube of Foundation in a Double Fanucci game, lost same said Cube in a game of Strip Grue, Fire, Water, and then was foreclosed on his property.

Jack retired to dinner theater, but after sixty years, he finally landed his big part in *Great Underground Adventure III*. (Parts I and II are still in development.) Since then, Jack has grown in reputation as the model Adventurer. His parents are proud, too, as no one suspects their prodigy's adventure disability. For Jack's part, he finally earned enough to fulfill his dream—owning a pawn shop.

Ultimately, though, this was reduced to Jack spending many hours spinning Adventurer's tales over the counter of his small pawn shop. His life was the envy of many a novice adventurer who stumbled into his shop, yet Jack himself had nothing to show for his difficult life. He was always late with his Inquisition taxes, and always fined for some trivial disrespect—for not displaying the proper insignia, the proper signs, closing according to the Inquisition Curfews and Inquisition Holidays, etc. However much he hated day to day life in Port Foozle, Jack was sufficiently embittered from the search for the exotic Flathead who had so besotted him, to remain an impartial bystander to the campaign of the Grand Inquisitor. He was, in short, retired...

AΠ ADVEΠTVRER IΠ PORT FOOZLE

Or so he swore to one such *ADVENTURER*, a scurvy looking sort, who happened into his shop in violation of the curfews of Port Foozle. However, when the Adventurer returned with nothing to show but an old brass lantern, Jack shoved him out of his shop, and swore to keep his distance. For the lamp was not just any lamp, but a magic lantern. And, as the legend goes, the Adventurer was not a knave, but a good soul, with an eye for Magic.

The Adventurer soon fell into the companionship of three Totems—none other than Lucy Flathead, the Griff, and the Brogmoid. Dalboz himself, once his captivity was discovered in the old brass lantern, oversaw the posse with what limited respect a bodiless voice could command.

The group dynamic was interesting, to say the least; Dalboz was hungry and bitter and betrayed—skeptical as to whether the GI could even be stopped, and in as foul a mood as any fellow stuffed in a lantern of that size was likely to be.

Lucy, for herself, was not accustomed to taking orders from a man, and found the arcane nature of Dalboz's Magicall knowledge, when combined with the insane nature of his utilitarian uselessness, somewhat aggravating.

The Griff liked nothing better than to order about the Brog, duping him into performing his own share of the work and more, and then blaming the Brog when these suggestions backfired.

The Brog didn't mind; he simply liked to talk with the twittering birds and the chirping insects, and instinctively find his way throughout the Underground, as he had since his was a pup. He was content just to look at Lucy, though more than anything he wished he could touch her.

Together, the party came across creatures and sights that would not be believed, were they to be described in length in this volume...

But they cannot be described, as they exist only Underground, and everyone knows that the Underground has long been sealed, and is without population or adventure. And they cannot be described, for they are Magicall, and everyone knows that Magic is dead, and powerless.

All Hail the Grand Inquisitor of Zork!

At this point, the pages became blacked out, and stamped with the following CEN-SORED stamp, patented by FROBOZZ ELECTRIC, makers of at least 39 different varieties of electrical and mechanical censorship devices. I believe I shall burn this book now. Yes, I think that would be best. Indeed... What book?

Chapter IV: The Walkthrough

Act I: Port Foozle and Elsewhere

You begin your noble quest at a crossroads. The sign in front of you points left towards Port Foozle, and right towards... Elsewhere.

The elsewhere that it refers to is the old Steppinthrax Monastery; headquarters of the Frobozz Electric Company and the Magic Inquisition. But we don't need to know that yet. Behind the sign, an unnamed path leads to a remote, nondescript well. But we don't need to know that yet either. For now, just head into Port Foozle.

The Sign Outside Port Foozle.

THE OUTSKIRTS OF FOOZLE

Welcome to lovely Port Foozle; home of one washed up Antharia Jack, an over-possessive fish, and a whole lot of silly, scared (or perhaps scared silly) townspeople. Don't worry, they're harmless, and this is a good space to familiarize yourself with how the game works.

There are a few things you can do at this point. You could go meet Antharia Jack at the Pawn Shack across from the dock. He'll just tell you to get lost, though. You could walk down the street and introduce yourself to the townspeople. Try it. You'll find they're a little hung up on this whole Inquisition thing, and will undoubtedly respond with some derivation of the phrase, "Go Away!"

You could head towards the dock and meet Marvin the Mythical Goatfish. But he's going through some tough times emotionally, and is wistful for the days when magic wasn't a four-letter word. Or whatever. He seems like he'd just rather be alone.

Man, what is it with everybody in this town?

The Inquisition Occupied Township of Port Foozle

Hint

Ice Chest Puzzle

One thing that might be worth your time would be to take a closer look at the fish market. In front of the fish market, there's the ice display case near the

The Fish Market's Last Fish.

dock. On the ice is some sort of large Herring and what looks like a six-ringed plastic can holder with a can of Mead. To the right of the ice display case, and closer to the street, the fish market's compulsory Inquisition speaker system is mounted on a wall. It's main dial control displays a variety of sound settings. Try taking the fish from the ice chest and seeing what happens. Then try playing with the speaker control dial. There should be three settings—"Any Lower and You'll Be Totemized!", "Just the Same As Everybody Else's", and "That's the Spirit!"

Solution

ICE CHEST PUZZLE

So you couldn't handle the first puzzle in the game, huh? Let's just chalk that one up to lack of experience and not worry about it. The fish market lady—a real charmer, isn't she?—stops you from taking her fish because every time you touch it, she hears the alarm going off. You can't turn the alarm off, but you can drown it out.

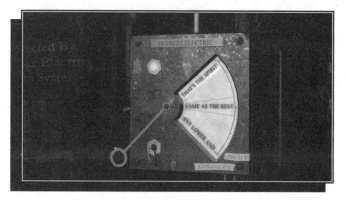

The Inquisition Loudspeaker's Volume Control.

Go to the speaker control dial and turn it up to its highest setting. When you reach for the fish now, she won't be able to hear the alarm, and thus, won't give you a hard time. All she'll hear is the booming broadcast of Inquisition Propaganda. But don't try to take anything until you hear the broadcast playing, or she'll bust you.

So You Reached for the Fish...

But you couldn't pick it up, could you? Don't worry, it's not just a dead herring, it's a red herring. Get it? You can't do anything with the fish. You don't want the fish. Forget the fish. Get over it. Pick up the six-pack holder and the can of Mead instead. By the way, the location of that six-pack holder was a pretty blatant clue for the next puzzle, so make sure not to overlook it.

Taken:
Six-Pack Holder
Can of Mead

The Dock Puzzle

Marvin the Mythical Goatfish.

You're now ready to deal with Marvin the Mythical Goatfish. Step up to the dock and click on the hook. Marvin should rise out of the water and give you a thorough tongue-lashing. Don't take it hard. He's sassy, and he's just trying to protect his grubby little corner of the undersea kingdom. Or is he? It almost seems as if—no, it couldn't be. Is Marvin trying to hide something? The only way to find out—without having an interactive conversation (which the designers of this game spared no inconvenience to avoid)—would be to get rid of him. Now how could you get rid of a pesky fish? It's like fishing, only in reverse.

Solution

THE DOCK PUZZLE

That's right. Strap your trusty six-pack holder onto the hook and let it drop into the murky depths. Hark! What's this? You caught the Goatfish, nearly strangled him, and ultimately ended up scaring him away. (If you were playing with your inventory in Port Foozle and tried to get Jack to open his door by showing him the six-pack holder, he would have told you, "That's one of those—you know—dangerous plastic thingies. Kills the fish").

TAKEN:	USED:
Lantern	**Six-Pack Holder**

You're all clear, kid. After the fish heads for deeper waters, you retrieve the crate he was protecting.

Hint

Factoid

The Adventurer's battered brass lantern is sort of a staple of the adventuring trade, at least in the Quendor / Frobozzica / Zork / The Great Underground Empire we've known over the years. Light from a lantern keeps you from being eaten by creatures inhabiting dark places. Historically, they have burnt for a period of time and then... sorry baby,

continues

THE LANTERN PUZZLE

The hook raises out of the water and drops a crate onto the dock. You open the crate and find a broken lantern inside. It doesn't seem to do much. But a lantern is an object of some significance to an Adventurer in the Zork universe. Perhaps there's someone who might be interested in such an item—perhaps someone located in this very town, with an expressly stated interest in acquiring said item. Perhaps he's near, waiting for just such an unassuming Adventurer as you to wander by and offer it to him. Give it a whirl. Go on. Take the lantern around and see what happens.

you're out of luck. All lanterns are not alike; you'll meet several varieties in this game alone. Other adventuring staples include: a book of matches, a rope, a map, an Elven sword, zorkmids... Okay I'm boring even myself here. Back to the game.

You find a broken lantern in a crate underneath the dock.

Solution

THE LANTERN PUZZLE

For Pete's sake, it's Jack! Offer the lantern to Antharia Jack in the pawn shack across the street. Just hand it to him—in other words, take the lantern from your inventory and click it on Jack's door—he'll gladly let you in.

Of course, he'll gladly kick you out, sans lantern, moments later. It's for your own good, he'll explain. Yeah, right. Your own good, and his.

FACTOID

By the way, look at his clothes. Look at the Fedora. Could you tell Laird Malamed, the Director of ZGI, is a real Indiana Jones fan? What gave that away?

Congratulations. You've just witnessed the first video clip of the game, and in it, you learned that your lantern is magic—but magic is dangerous, and nobody will help you because it's curfew and they all fear the dreaded Inquisition. And you lost your lamp.

Antharia Jack tries to fix your lantern.

USED:
Lantern

BUT BEFORE YOU GET THE BOOT

TAKEN:
Cigar

Don't forget to take one of the auto-lighting cigars from Jack's box. You have a limited window of opportunity here, so don't miss it. (Well, if you do miss it, you can return to Jack's and he'll give you one.)

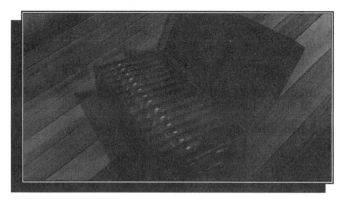

Have a cigar.

BACK WHERE YOU STARTED

"Trust me. You don't want it." says Antharia Jack. Here's a free hint. Don't trust him. You want it. You want to get the lantern back. He won't let you in again. But maybe, if you make enough of a commotion, you can get him to come out and stay out for good. But how? Check your inventory. See if you have the ingredients for a diversion.

Solution

BACK WHERE YOU STARTED

See that cigar in your inventory? It's auto lighting when you want to use it. Now you just need to find something to burn. See that stand packed with Inquisition merchandise off in the distance? Go check it out. See that highly flammable Grand Inquisitor doll? Set it on fire. Someone will yell fire and an alarm will sound. Jump in the nearby empty barrel and watch through the hole in its side. The guards won't see you. Go on. Hide in the barrel... quick!

Through the side of the barrel you see the second video clip of the game, where you meet the dreaded Vice Under Secretary Wartle and his henchman (wait, can a henchman have a henchman?) and watch him arrest—Jack! Jack,

FACTOID

Yes, behind that curly moustachio that's Rip Taylor as the scary, scary Vice Under-Secretary Wartle. Even if you aren't a fan of full motion video, you have to admit, if there has to be video in a game, it really should be video of Rip Taylor. No confetti, though.

USED:
Cigar

69

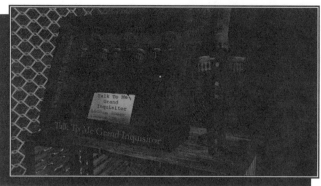

with his cigar smoking habit, has been arrested instead of you!

He's not going to be too happy about this.

Make sure to hide once you set fire to the Grand Inquisitor doll.

HIT THE ROAD, JACK

Where were we? Oh yes. You duck into the barrel and watch as Wartle leads Jack away, leaving his shop completely unattended. It's now available for all your pilfering needs. You're a looter, except you're only after one thing. Go inside and take the lantern. That voice you hear inside it is the disembodied Dungeon Master. He wants very badly for you to get underground.

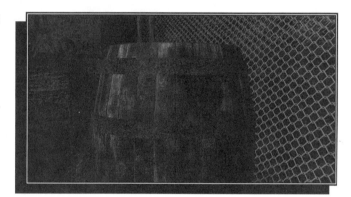

Antharia Jack takes the wrap for your crime.

TAKEN:
Lantern

You're now done with Port Foozle. Feel free to look around, talk to people, and listen to the uplifting messages of the Inquisition for as long as you want, then head on back to the sign at the crossroads.

BOY, WOULD MALVEAUX BE P.O.'D IF HE SAW THIS

Head directly away from Port Foozle at the sign. Follow the Elsewhere arrow toward the rock wall in the distance and you'll soon find yourself swept up a mountain path.

Once you are standing in front of the old Steppinthrax Monastery (Remember this place? If you played *Zork Nemesis*, it should look familiar.) It's been thoroughly converted since the days of Zorkastrianism, but it's the same dark and nasty place.

The old Steppinthrax Monastery is now the headquarters for the Inquisition.

This brief field trip up the hill is only a dark and nasty prelude of yes, dark and nasty things to come, so there's not much to do here. Look around and read the signs, then pull the noose off of the "Totemized Daily" billboard—because you can, and if you can, you'll need it. That is, as you probably know, the governing logic in this Empire.

TAKEN:
Noose

Being Totemized is a Very Bad Thing.

"Get Underground"

There's only one place left to go. Follow the path behind the crossroads sign and you'll find yourself in a clearing occupied only by an abandoned well. If you talk to the Dungeon Master, he'll clearly state and restate, and then state some more, his desire for you to go underground. You have all the tools to do so. Figure it out. There's only one place in Foozle that leads under the ground... Well?

It may look innocent, but this well is your doorway to the Great Underground Empire.

"Get Underground"

Well, indeed! Employing your full capacity for deductive reasoning, you tie the rope to the well and climb down. With the functioning lantern in your inventory, the well-bottom won't be shrouded in darkness, and you can avoid being eaten by a grue.

Now we're getting somewhere.

> USED:
> **Rope**
> **Lantern**

A Not-So-Brief Debriefing

The Dungeon Master has a lot to talk about. He's been jammed up in this lamp and now he's looking for a little action and a few good adventurers. But he'll settle for you. He gives you a quick run-down of who he is and how he ended up in a lamp, then introduces you to Y'Gael. Y'Gael is sort of a ditz. However, being the generous enchantress that she is, Y'Gael leaves you with a spell book. Take it. Read it. Learn it. Use it.

Open up your spell book and the Dungeon Master tells you all about spells and spell-casting. You start off with three spells: Rezrov, Igram, and Voxam. Rezrov you use right away. Igram can be used in a few places, the first of which is very close by. Voxam, however, isn't useful for quite some time.

The Dungeon Master instructs you to select the Rezrov spell and cast it on the door. Do that, and the door opens.

> *Tip: Take note of the symbols next to the spells and you can select them quickly from the spell menu bar in the upper-right corner of your game screen.*

You can click on the staircase now to descend, but before you do that, take a look in the bucket to the right of the door. There's a subway token inside. Pick it up and toss it into your inventory.

> *Note: In case you're wondering about your rope, you will need it later, but for now, with it tied at the top of the well, and the DM warning you not to climb up, you must leave it be.*

You're all set. Click on the banister of the staircase. You'll quickly find that the staircase has a life of its own, and it doesn't much tolerate being trampled on.

After a quick ride down the Dragon Staircase, you find yourself at the beginning of the second leg of the game.

FACTOID

Do you recognize the voice? It's Micheal McKeon. Check the characters section for more of a run down. Do you realize that both Lenny and Squiggy (that voice on the Inquisition Loudspeaker) are now in this game?

What's this door doing at the bottom of a well?

Act II: The Underground

You've heard about it in legends of old. Here's the real thing. The magical, fantastical Great Underground Empire of Zork. There are lots of paths to follow and things to do in the environment that you've just entered. You don't need to do everything just yet, but you're welcome to give it a try.

In case of Adventure

Fortunately, someone thought to leave you adequately prepared for an occasion just like this.

The most important thing not to miss on your first pass through this environment is the emergency case on the wall, left of the dragon staircase. Go to the close-up and open up the case.

When you click on the sword or map inside the case, you discover that they're stuck firmly to the case's backing. No matter how hard you try, the items just won't come loose.

Don't let yourself get too vexed by this one. The solution is simple. Just follow the directions.

Act II: The Underground

Solution

In Case of Adventure

Open the case. Pick the hammer up. Close the case. Smash the glass with the hammer. Pull the items out of the case through the glass. Get it? It's like, a joke.

TAKEN:
Sword
Map

Factoid

Mason Deming, the Lead Scriptor on ZGI, came up with that baby at a late night pizza design review session when he really just wanted to be home sleeping. Now, see, whoever said programmers aren't creative?

First Stab at the Umbrella Tree

If you look to the left of the case, you'll discover the purple umbrella tree. You don't have what you need to get the umbrellas to open yet, but if you think for a moment, you should recall something else you can do to the tree.

That's right. Cast Igram—the spell that turns purple things invisible—on the tree and you'll SEE the spell scroll stored inside one of the buds. Notice the stress on the word SEE. You'll get to TAKE it much later on.

You don't have the spell you need to solve the umbrella tree yet.

USED:
Igram

Veer Left at the Fork in the Road

Head away from the tree, towards the open area in the distance, and you are standing in the center of the Underground Crossroads. This is the main junction for the entire game. Four paths lead out from this point. You've already taken care of one. The remaining three comprise the rest of Act II.

The path in front of you takes you to GUE Tech, once the leading magic institution of Zork. The path to the right leads to the Great Underground Subway, also known as the Underground Underground. These are both places that you will enter and explore in time, but for the critical path of the game, it's fastest to take a left and head towards the wooden door leading to the Dungeon Master's Lair. Before you head that way, though, walk to the center and check out the weird looking machine wedged into the ground. It's called a Frobozz Magic Teleportation Station.

It can't be used now, but by walking up to it and placing your map in the wide, horizontal slot, it is activated as a place you can jump back to. An overhead view of the area

USED:
Map

you're occupying appears on the screen. You can push the left and right arrows, but they won't do anything yet. Just take your map back out and walk away.

Hint

Thwarting the Rank Undergrowth

Look, an open door. Unfortunately, it might as well be closed because as you step closer you are face to face with an impassably dense clump of vegetation. Impassable—that is—without the help of a very trusty and recently acquired inventory item...

The rank undergrowth prevents eastward movement.

Solution

Thwarting the Rank Undergrowth

Sheesh! Nothing gets past you, does it? With nary a moment to contemplate, you swiftly draw your Elven sword of great antiquity and use it to vanquish the foliage. (Don't worry, they do get harder).

Used:
Sword

Better Lairs and Gardens

Factoid

Spell books were first introduced to the Zork Series in Enchanter (which would have been called Zork IV if they had called it that). As in Zork Grand Inquisitor, you gain more spells in Enchanter by finding scrolls and then Gnustoing them into your spell book. Due to recent technological improvements in Spell books, this is now an automatic process.

You are now standing on the Dungeon Master's front lawn. This would be trespassing, were you not accompanied by the property's owner, who is stuffed in a brown sack and slung over your shoulder. Granted, there may be legal ramifications to doing that as well, but you don't have time to stand around debating them right now.

Open the gardening shed right in front of you and pull out the Throck scroll and the shovel lying at the bottom. These are the Dungeon Master's gardening tools. Since he doesn't have much use for them, they're yours to keep. The Throck scroll should be immediately Gnustoed into your inventory.

Instead of going back the way that you came, head towards the house in the distance and walk around to the back. There is a Teleportation Station there. Slide your map in and press the left or right arrow so that the Underground Crossroads location appears on the viewer. When it does, press the glowing circle on the screen. You are magically teleported to the corresponding station in that location.

The Dungeon Master's Gardening Tools.

BACK TO THE UNDERGROUND CROSSROADS

Appearing near the center of the crossroads, you take a step back and get your bearings (making sure to take your map back before walking away). The next place you need to visit is GUE Tech, which is straight down the path, a little to the left of the Teleportation Station that you just materialized in front of.

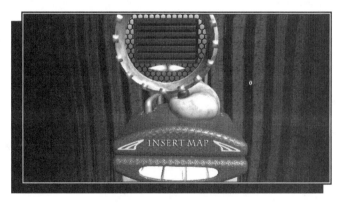

There are several more of these stations located throughout the underground, and you will find them a highly effective method for avoiding the tedium of navigation.

Anyway, walk down the path to GUE Tech.

Use the Teleportation Stations to jump through the underground with greater efficiency.

If You Can't Handle This One, Go Back to Myst

Now head down the path leading to the GUE Tech entrance. The door is magically sealed, forbidding access to those without basic spellcasting ability. Yessiree, basic spellcasting ability is all you'll need to get through this door. Ahem...

Prove your worthiness to enter the ancient spell casting university.

Solution

If You Can't Handle This One, Go Back to Myst

USED:
Rezrov

Remember that thing you did to that door a while back? Do it again. Cast Rezrov, walk through the doorway, and you're all done.

CHEATING ON THE ENTRANCE EXAM, PART I

You're standing outside the most renowned spellcasting academy in the entire Moss League. Suffice it to say, you can't just waltz right in the front door. You can square-dance in, but that would require careful orchestration and a Local Area Network.

Kidding.

You must pass the three entrance exams. The Dungeon Master tells you all about them, but he won't tell you how to solve them. Which is why you bought this book.

You must make one logical, continuous image out of the three rows of pictures on each pillar. On the first pillar, concentrate on the top and bottom rows. Spin the top once-around, then take a look at the bottom. Look for something on the bottom that relates indirectly to something on the top. It won't be a part of the same object, but something that would logically be in the same image. Once you've found the top and bottom images, spin the middle around until you've found the piece that looks right with the other two.

CHEATING ON THE ENTRANCE EXAM, PART I

Spin the top row until you find the picture of the volcano. Spin the bottom until you find the lava flowing under the bridge. Spin the middle one until the puzzle stops and cuts to the victory animation. The pillar slams down and is covered by a small bridge that extends like a telescope. Walk across to the next pillar.

Spin the pillar's rows the find the right image.

CHEATING ON THE ENTRANCE EXAM, PART II

The second pillar consists of a series of obelisks, broken up into segments for you to re-assemble. To solve the pillar, pay close attention to the shadows and the directions they face on both the ground, and the obelisks themselves. You also can eliminate a few obelisks by noticing simple visual clues.

To solve this one faster, notice which way the shadows are facing.

Solution

CHEATING ON THE ENTRANCE EXAM, PART II

You want the narrow, four-sided obelisk that looks like the Washington monument. It has a large "Z" at the top and a shadow on the right side. Once you find it, the bottomless pit in front of you turns to shadow and you'll be able to walk across to the third and final pillar.

Hint

CHEATING ON THE ENTRANCE EXAM, PART III

Welcome to the third and final pillar. This one has several complete images in it that are easy to create. None of them, however, will get you into GUE Tech. The correct answer is not to look for matching backgrounds.

You're trying to make a window that you can crawl through to enter the University.

CHEATING ON THE ENTRANCE EXAM, PART III

The correct answer is to find the three window pieces placed into different background images and bring them together. Once the window is formed, the background fades away and you can crawl through into GUE Tech.

The GUE Tech Rotunda is one of the richest environments in the game.

Hint

PAY NO ATTENTION TO THE INCREDIBLE GRAPHICS, YOU'VE GOT WORK TO DO

You're in the GUE Tech rotunda. No oggling! Sure the environment is beautiful. Sure the fountain is amazing. But you can't just sit there lollygagging while thousands of Port Foozilians suffer. You've got an Inquisition to stop. Okay, fine. Oggle. Lollygag, even. You can sit there for a year if you want, it won't change a thing

Let's just hope that really is dirt.

(aside from the screen-burn). You could play around—try out the vending machines—if you had the coinage. Sorry. For now, you're stuck window shopping.

When you're done, turn around and head out the front door. You'll find your-self on the far side of the third pillar. When you turn around outside you'll dis-cover that the University isn't where it should be. As the Dungeon Master explains, GUE Tech exists in the Ethereal Plains of Atrii. The only way to get in is through the window on the third pillar. And the only way to get to where you are is by walking out the front door.

HEY, FREE DIRT!

Now walk up the staircase to where the University's rotunda should be and look at the pile of free dirt to the right of the fountain. While the dirt is indeed free, you unfortunately have no use for it. You do have use for something inside the dirt, but you're far too concerned with your appearance to go digging in that mess with your hands.

HEY, FREE DIRT!

Pull out your shovel and go digging in the dirt. You'll find the Kendall scroll (Simplify Instructions), which will be auto-gnustoed and ready for use at the click of a button. That's it for now. As with the Dungeon Master's Lair, there's a lot more to do, but it has to wait.

TAKEN:	USED:
Kendall	**Shovel**
	Map

For now, step over to the Teleportation Station nearby and slide your map in. Select the overhead image of the Underground Crossroads, click on the image of the station in that environment, and you'll go straight...

BACK TO THE UNDERGROUND CROSSROADS, YET AGAIN

You're back in the crossroads for a third time. Face the Teleportation Station that you just materialized in front of and head to the right. Go down the only path you've yet to take. It leads to the Great Underground Subway entrance.

WERE YOU PAYING ATTENTION?

At the entrance to the Great Underground Subway you'll find your course obstructed again, this time by a turnstile. There's a slot next to the turnstile with an appetite that clearly needs to be sated before access to the subway can be gained. The puzzle here isn't in figuring out what needs to be put in the slot, but in finding the object to begin with.

You did pick up that subway token, didn't you?

You've already passed through the location where the item is. And if, in fact, you've been following the guide's directions, you should already have it. It's easy to miss though, so you may have to go back and get it before you move on.

Were You Paying Attention?

The subway token is lying in the bucket at the bottom of the well. If you haven't already picked it up, go back and get it. Once you slide it in, you'll be able to glide down the escalator and into the first of several subway stations. You get an all-day pass, so you need only one subway token.

> USED:
> **Subway token**

Navigating the Underground Underground

Welcome to the Great Underground Subway system, or as it's informally known, the Underground Underground. First, head to the center of the station and glance at the add for the Old Scratch Lottery Game. Some money would be good about now. Also, there are references to Hades, so that may be a clue about where to get a lottery ticket.

As for the Underground, it's by far the fastest way to get around, barring spells, potions, and all other forms of sorcerous spatial manipulation. But alas, its usefulness is hindered by a couple of rather serious flaws.

First off, it's somewhat difficult to navigate through the myriad of disconnected subway lines and

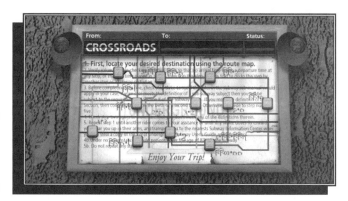

You won't get anywhere by just pushing buttons here.

reach any sort of intended destination. And since the subway won't pick you up unless a target location is entered, few people were ever able to get on board.

As for the second flaw... We'll get to that later.

You can walk up to the subway map and start pressing buttons in the hopes of finding somewhere to go. But that gets you nowhere.

Navigating the Underground Underground

Casting the Kendall spell on the map— now that gets you places. The map becomes vastly simplified, and you can easily gain access to several new locations.

The only one you need to concern yourself with now is the Hades stop. Press

Used:
Kendall

that button and approach the platform to await the next car.

Oh, and about that second flaw—well, you'll see.

A Quick Jaunt Across the Hades Waiting Room

You arrive at the Hades subway stop, which also doubles as the waiting room for passage across the River Styx. Walk up to the skeleton sitting on the bench and look in its hand. There's a lottery ticket resting there. Pilfer the Old Scratch lottery ticket and drop it in your inventory.

FACTOID

There's apparently some confusion over the exact conceptual origin of the place called Hades. It's commonly accepted that the first mention of Hades appeared in a certain text-based adventure game entitled, Zork: The Great Underground Empire. However, some "academics" continue to insist that it was first referred to in the mythology of some far-off, ancient civilization that nobody cares about. While the latter theory may seem valid to those with only a limited knowledge of historical literature, it is clearly impossible, as text-based games had not yet been invented in ancient times.

Now take a look at the book setting next to him. It contains a few hints for a puzzle that you'll encounter later on.

> TAKEN:
> **Old Scratch lottery ticket**

This poor gentleman apparently died reading a book in the nude.

Hint

OLD SCRATCH'S GAMBLE

Go to your inventory screen, pick up the Old Scratch lottery ticket, and drop it into your close-up viewer. It blows up to full-screen. This is a scratch-off lottery game with a very severe twist. If you win, you get a 500 zorkmid bill (zorkmids are, of course, the currency of Zork). If you lose, you're damned for eternity. Don't worry, though. If you move slowly and think before you scratch, you should be fine.

Your goal is to navigate your way through the maze, from the starting point to the treasure in the center, without making any wrong moves. The reason the maze looks all disjointed and scrambled is because each row of blocks has been rotated by a multiple of 90 degrees. By rotating them back in your mind and checking a few blocks ahead to make sure your chosen path doesn't dead end, you should be able to find your way with little trouble.

☉ OLD SCRATCH'S GAMBLE

But if you do have a problem, you can look at this screen and find the correct path.

When you've made it to the center, the ticket dissolves and is replaced by a crisp 500 zorkmid bill. Click anywhere on the screen and the money is dumped into your inventory—and you return to the normal game.

For those of you with cheatin' hearts, here's the correct path to the center.

Note: You don't have to solve the Old Scratch lottery ticket inside the Hades subway station. You can go anywhere in the game and look at it, and it's still playable.

Keep walking away from where the subway dropped you off and you'll arrive at the shore of the River Styx. The red phone nearby may look tempting, but you don't need to solve that puzzle yet. Instead, turn to the Teleportation Station nearby and slide the map in. Push the right arrow until you see the overhead view of the fountain area in the GUE Tech exterior. Click on the image of the Teleportation Station in that environment and you'll instantly get beamed there.

Taken:	Used:
500 zorkmid bill	**Old Scratch lottery ticket**
	Map

Back to School

You're back in GUE Tech. Head towards the window on the third pillar and climb through to get back inside the university. You've got everything you need now to go all the way through this entire section of the game.

The Infinite Corridor

You need to shorten the Infinite Corridor.

Walk around the fountain in the center of the room and stand at the mouth of the long hallway extending out from the back of the rotunda. Take a look down that hall. It's really long, isn't it? Yep, really, really long. You can walk down it if you want. You'll find that it is, indeed, really, really, really long.

Okay, come back out of the hallway now and look at the plaque at the top of the entrance-way. Hmm, "The Infinite Corridor." That sounds like a problem. You really need to get to the end of that hallway. What could possibly fix this situation?

THE INFINITE CORRIDOR

Aha! Look again. The word "Infinite" is written in what magical color? Check your spell book and look for the spell that turns purple things invisible. Igram. Grand! Now cast Igram on the word "Infinite" to make it simply "The Corridor." Brilliant! The hallway may now be easily crossed. Quickly step into the hallway to make it a smallway, as the DM explains. What the DM does not explain is that this was part of the hazing procedures at GUE Tech. Many a student was flunked out for poor attendance because they could not get to their classes. If you wait too long to walk down the hall, the hallway reverts. However, once you walk into the smallway, it stays that way.

FACTOID

This is another place to see some wrong answers. Instead of casting Igram on Infinite, cast it on Corridor instead. Don't walk into this one—it's very cold in space. Once you solve the hallway you can cast Igram on Corridor, as well.

USED:
Igram

VENDING MACHINE HI-JINX

Before you go through the corridor there are several tasks to complete with the vending machines. The first one involves the change machine. There's a certain matter regarding one 500 zorkmid bill that could perhaps be handled quite appropriately by said machine. Slip the bill into the change machine and you'll find a large quantity of zorkmids awaiting collection in the dispenser bin. Pick them up and they'll automatically be dumped into a coin sack in your inventory screen.

This is where you get the endless supply of zorkmids that you'll be using throughout the game.

Taken:	Used:
A Great Number of zorkmids	**500 zorkmid bill**

More Fun With Vending Machines

Next, turn to the ice cream machine to the left of the change machine. Go into your inventory, take a zorkmid out of your sack and drop it into the coin slot on the machine. You can now open any one of the three doors on the machine. The first two are empty, but if you open the one on the right, you'll find one ice cream sandwich left inside. Take it out, then drop it in the close-up viewer in your inventory. The wrapper is removed and the ice cream melts instantly, but if you look on the inside of the wrapper, you'll discover that it contains a novelty Obidil scroll. The Dungeon Master explains that if you take it to the Spell Checker and run it through, it alters the scroll to make it a fully gnusto-able spell.

> *Note: You can press F9 to automatically grab a coin. Anything you were carrying is put back in your inventory for you.*

Taken:	Used:
Ice cream sandwich	**Zorkmid**
Obidil scroll	**Ice cream sandwich**

There's something behind one of these three doors.

Still More Fun With Vending Machines

Now turn all the way around and look at the candy machine on the far right. Put a zorkmid in and press any of the buttons. On second thought, just press the button labeled "8", as that is the only one that matters. As you'll notice, the package of Zork Rocks that you selected didn't make it out of the machine. They got stuck. If you put more zorkmids in and select it again, you'll just be draining your infinite supply of cash. You'll need to figure out some way to force the Zork Rocks out of the machine.

None of your spells or items can break the magically reinforced glass. If you look down at the bottom of the machine, you'll see the dispenser where the candy drops down to. Notice the round, almost nozzle-shaped design of the dispenser.

Those Zork Rocks on the second row are important.

Solution

STILL MORE FUN WITH VENDING MACHINES

There you go. Attach the perma-suck to the candy machine dispenser and it's a perfect fit. Without concerning yourself with how an 8-foot long mechanism of solid steel construction was stored in your beginning inventory sack, go ahead and activate it. It sucks the machine relentlessly until the Zork Rocks slide out and clog the suck-valve. Open up the side panel and take the Zork Rocks out of the machine. Unfortunately, this has rendered the perma-suck completely ineffective for further use. The Zork Rocks have shredded all the internal components. That's Frobozz Electric craftsmanship for you. Leave it here.

TAKEN:	USED:
Zork rocks	**Zorkmid**
	Perma-suck machine

STILL EVEN MORE FUN YET
WITH VENDING MACHINES

Now move on to the soda machine in the middle of the area. There are four different cola beverages that you can purchase by sliding a zorkmid into this machine, but since the machine is out of cups, none of them is actually attainable in a contained fluid form.

Remember what the bulletin board said? One of the items in this machine is half of a highly volatile mixture.

However, as you noticed from reading the bulletin board, one of the sodas in particular is known to have an extremely volatile and potentially useful effect when combined with a certain item that happens to be in your inventory.

Solution

STILL EVEN MORE FUN YET
WITH VENDING MACHINES

Drop the Zork Rocks into the cola dispenser area, slide a zorkmid into the machine and select Blam Classic. The Zork Rocks have now been corrupted, and will detonate in 45 seconds. If you're still reading this, you either have no concept of the severity of this situation, or you haven't actually done what's just been instructed. Perhaps it's better if you haven't. Finish reading this, then go ahead and do it.

Take the pulsing-red Zork Rocks and run down the once-infinite corridor (if you neglected to complete the Infinite Corridor puzzle, you're pretty much screwed at this point). When you get to the end, you'll find a wall of 12 lockers facing you. One of the locker doors (the second one from the left in the middle row) is bent open a crack, but is still shut. Slide the Zork Rocks into that locker and wait for them to explode. The locker door will fly open, allowing you access to the Dungeon Master's old locker.

Okay, now that you know what to do, put the book down and do it.

USED:
Glowing Zork Rocks
Zorkmid

Once you blast the door off, avoid the urge to look inside just yet. Instead, return head back to the candy machine, pop another zorkmid inside, and press candy 11. It won't fall, but something else will occur elsewhere. Now head back down the hall to the lockers.

Inside the Lockers

If you stand at the end of the once-infinite corridor, you should see two locker doors open. You just opened one of them by detonating the Zork Rocks, and the other you opened when you selected number 11 on the candy machine. The locker doors are actually connected to the candy machine buttons, so that pressing any of the buttons opens a locker in the corresponding position (button number 1 opens the upper-left locker, 2 opens the next one over, and so on). You need to open only locker 11 though, so don't worry about the others. (You couldn't open number 6 without the Zork Rocks because the candy machine button was broken.)

Look inside the Dungeon Master's locker—the second one from the left on the middle row—and take the student ID card lying inside.

Then switch over to the bottom-right locker—the Grand Inquisitor's old locker from his days as a talentless wizard-in-training. He's got a stack of cheat sheets and books to help him scrape through his classwork. Some of them are conveniently relevant to what you'll need to do later on. Read the books on spell manufacturing and time tunnels.

Yannick's also got some anti-anxiety medication that he used to keep him from becoming a megalomaniacal tyrant. Pick up the blue Prozork tablet and drop it in your inventory.

The Dungeon Master's Locker from his days at GUE Tech.

THE WIZARD BELBOZ

Before you enter the Spell Labs, head down the three other corridors that lead out from this location. At the end of each one you'll find a mural that pictures one of the three lost artifacts. When you click on each one, the Wizard Belboz chimes in and explains what the artifact is, where it came from, the power that it contains, and where it was last seen.

These lectures are entirely superfluous to your completion of the game, but they do fill in a few holes and provide some backstory on the Zork universe. Go ahead and check them out.

FACTOID

The Wizard Belboz is a character from the Enchanter trilogy. In his day—that being a period of 42 years that took place several centuries into his life—he was Guildmaster for the Accardi chapter of the Guild of Enchanters. A wise and gifted sorcerer, he was later promoted to oversee the Enchanter's Guild as a whole, a title that allowed him to give guidance to a talented

continues

99

young apprentice. The very same apprentice defeated Krill and Jearr, then succeeded Belboz as the next head of the Enchanter's Guild, and later set in motion the sordid debacle that led to the banishing of magic from Zork. Which led to an age of tyranny, highlighted by the megalomaniacal rule of the Grand Inquisitor. Which, in turn, led to the Dungeon Master getting stuck in a lantern. Which led to you having to lug him around the underground in an attempt to undo the mess caused by Belboz giving bad guidance in the first place.

But that's all water under the bridge.

You're not into the lab yet, though. You still have to get past the invisible six-armed guard. He's mighty feisty. You can try attacking him with your sword, but that would be stupid. He has five more of them than you do, and his swordsmanship far outclasses yours.

The Coconut of Quendor is one of the three lost artifacts of Zork.

Hint

The Invisible Six-Armed Guard

Step up to the Spell Labs door and slide the Dungeon Master's student ID card into the card slot. The door opens and you can step through.

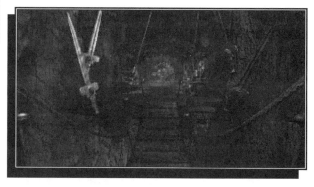

The invisible six-armed guard has a distinct advantage at hand-to-hand combat.

You could try casting Igram on him, but somebody already beat you to it. You could cycle through all your inventory items. Nothing works. You've got to think of another way to get rid of him.

The Invisible Six-Armed Guard

Cut the rope bridge with your sword and send him straight down into the ravine below.

At the moment, you're stuck because taking out the guard took out the bridge as well. You need to do some more exploring. Head over to the teleportation station and select Crossroads, then go to the Underground and send yourself to Flood Control Dam #3.

Whoops. You've just destroyed the only route to the spell lab. Now what?

USED:
Sword

Flood Control Dam #3

After checking up on Jack, you end your subway ride near the famous Flood Control Dam #3. Renowned for its amazing ability to sneak its way into adventure game sequels, the Flood Control Dam is one of the best-known tourist attractions in Zork. Unfortunately, for the purposes of this puzzle, the centuries-old remnant of Dimwit Flathead's excessive rule must be put on the chopping block.

Take a look at the book on the counter next to the FCD controls. It contains some history on the dam, as well as the very important Golgatem scroll, which is hidden in between the pages. Pull the scroll out and Gnusto it into your spell book.

Getting all these doors to close at the same time isn't as easy as it looks.

You need to get the water that is blocked by the dam flowing through the empire. To do that, you must break the dam. To break the dam, you must close all four sluice doors at the same time (as the book on the nearby table explains). To close all four sluice doors... you must do something very clever, because pushing the open/close buttons by themselves isn't going to work.

FLOOD CONTROL DAM #3

Factoid

Did you try to cast Golgatem on the Dam? Pretty neat bridge, isn't it? However, it does you absolutely no good whatsoever. This is one of a number of "wrong answers" in the game. The designers

continues

The control buttons for the dam have some weird dependencies attached to them. Pressing one button that seems to correspond directly to one of the sluice doors invariably affects another gate as well. Since all four doors behave in this way, it's impossible to get all four closed at the same time—unless you close one of the doors by unnatural means, disrupting the normal pattern of dependencies.

include wrong answers to reward players who try things that make sense, but don't actually solve puzzles. Many of these wrong answers can be found by casting spells on the characters you meet or handing them different objects. Experiment as you explore, but it's always a good idea to save before trying anything really dangerous—like jumping in a pit.

Cast *Rezrov* on any one of the four sluice gates, and it will suddenly become possible—nay, easy—to rearrange them so that they're all closed at the same time. Do so. Make it so.

The dam bursts shortly thereafter, and one cut-scene later, water flows through new, unexpected, yet enormously relevant areas of the underground.

Taken:	Used:
Golgatem	**Rezrov**

Factoid

Golgatem is named for the Golden Gate Bridge.

Hint

Moss Doesn't Just Grow on Trees

Take a step back towards the subway map and look at the pipe running down the nearby wall. At the bottom, where the pipe empties out through the grate, you'll notice a tiny bit of moss growing out. This is Moss of Mareilon, as the Dungeon Master explains. It's not enough to scrape off as it is, but...

Moss of Mareilon can often be found growing in drain pipes.

Moss Doesn't Just Grow on Trees

If you cast Throck on it, it'll grow to a much more practical size. Go ahead and grab it.

Lastly, slip a zorkmid into the souvenir zorkmid to Letter Opener machine to gather a rather nifty memento of this once revered tourist spot. Return to the spell labs armed with Golgatem.

Taken:	Used:
Moss of Mareilon	**Throck**
Letter Opener	**Zorkmid**

Back in the Spell Labs

Used:
Golgatem

Cast the Golgatem spell to build a new bridge across the ravine, then walk across into the Spell Labs.

Note: *Did you notice in the FCD book the anecdote about GUE Tech being flooded once? The effect of breaking the dam has been to get water flowing through the Spell Labs ravine, which is beneficial because Golgatem only works over a body of water.*

THE BEBURTT CONUNDRUM

Turn to your right and take the parchment out of the crate. It's an un-imbued Beburtt scroll. This would be a highly useful scroll to have, were it working.

To get it working, you're going to need to place it on five of the six imbuing tables in the proper order. To find the order, you need to read the spell manufacturing book that was in Yannick's locker and solve the logic problem contained inside.

The book tells you that light and dark spells alternate, and if you look up Beburtt at the beginning of the spell glossary, it tells you that Beburtt begins with Origination. This means that the second table must be one of the lights; either elucidation, interpretation, or modification.

	1	2	3	4	5
Light:					
Elucidation	X		X		X
Interpretation	X		X		X
Modification	X		X		X
Dark:					
Transmogrification	X	X		X	
Origination	O	X	X	X	X
Replication	X	X		X	

The book also tells you that replication and interpretation must be used, and that replication precedes interpretation. This means that replication cannot be the last table in the process. But since it cannot be immediately before or after another dark table, and origination is already in the first spot, it must be either the third or fifth table in the process. We just ruled out the fifth, so replication must come third, followed immediately after by interpretation. This leaves only one dark table left for the fifth spot; therefore, transmogrification must come last.

	I	2	3	4	5
Light:					
Elucidation	X		X	X	X
Interpretation	X	X	X	O	X
Modification	X		X	X	X
Dark:					
Transmogrification	X	X	X	X	O
Origination	O	X	X	X	X
Replication	X	X	O	X	X

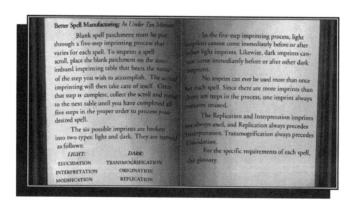

Better Spell Manufacturing: In Under Ten Minutes

Blank spell parchment must be put through a five-step imprinting process that varies for each spell. To imprint a spell scroll, place the blank parchment on the auto-imbued imprinting table that bears the name of the step you wish to accomplish. The actual imprinting will then take care of itself. Once that step is complete, collect the scroll and move to the next table until you have completed all five steps in the proper order to process your desired spell.

The six possible imprints are broken into two types: light and dark. They are named as follows:

LIGHT:
ELUCIDATION
INTERPRETATION
MODIFICATION

DARK:
TRANSMOGRIFICATION
ORIGINATION
REPLICATION

In the five-step imprinting process, light imprints cannot come immediately before or after other light imprints. Likewise, dark imprints cannot come immediately before or after other dark imprints.

No imprint can ever be used more than once for each spell. Since there are more imprints than there are steps in the process, one imprint always remains unused.

The Replication and Interpretation imprints are always used, and Replication always precedes Interpretation. Transmogrification always precedes Elucidation.

For the specific requirements of each spell, the glossary.

Solve this logic problem to learn how to make the Beburtt Spell.

Solution

The Beburtt Conundrum

The only spot remaining is the second. It can either be modification or elucidation. The book tells us that elucidation is preceded by transmogrification, but it doesn't say that elucidation must be used, as it specifically states with replication and interpretation. Since transmogrification appears last, and can't really precede anything, there is a clear conflict making it impossible to use elucidation. This means that modification must go in the second spot.

Therefore, the order of the five tables must be Origination, Modification, Replication, Interpretation, and Transmogrification.

Of course, you could also figure that out through trial and error, but it would take you a while.

The Smartass Solution

There's another way of solving the Beburtt puzzle that would occur only to the extremely clever or the extremely lazy. Remember the Kendall spell that you picked up earlier? You can cast it on the book in the locker and the spell manufacturing instructions are replaced by the correct order of the tables.

Once you've run Beburtt through all the tables, slide it into the Spell Checker so that it can be Gnustoed into your spell book.

You can also take the Obidil scroll that you picked up from the ice cream machine and run it through at this point. You now have two new spells.

Taken:	Used:
Un-imbued Beburtt parchment	**Un-imbued Beburtt parchment**
Beburtt	
Obidil	

Unfinished Business With the Umbrella Tree

When you're done with the Spell Checker, turn around and walk back across the bridge. Go to the Teleportation Station on the cliff edge and beam back to the cross- roads. Now head over to the umbrella tree that you left unfin- ished ages ago. You need to get the umbrellas to open so that the spell hidden inside one of them will fall out. In your travels you have acquired a spell that can help resolve this situation.

Trick the umbrellas and you'll get the scroll out.

Factoid

Laird Malamed, the director of Zork Grand Inquisitor, named Beburtt, which creates the illusion of inclement weather by making a thunder sound effect, in honor of the Sound Effects Designer, Ben Burtt. Ben, besides being a wonderfully nice guy, also has

continues

Unfinished Business With the Umbrella Tree

Cast Beburtt on the umbrella tree and take the Zimdor scroll that falls to the ground. The Zimdor spell triplicates quantities of intoxicating libations. You can't Gnusto it because it can only be cast once, but you can get rid of it quick- ly if you know what to cast it on.

a few Academy Awards for work on the Star Wars and Indiana Jones films.

Hint

Vegetation Medication

Don't get too close to the snapdragon.

Once you're finished with the umbrella tree, head back into the Dungeon Master's garden. On the left side of the garden, a short ways in, you'll find a snapdragon. You need to take it. Once again, attacking it with your sword will prove fruitless. You have to give this some thought. The book that you'll find inside the Dungeon Master's house would help you figure out what to do, but we're not in the Dungeon Master's house, are we? You should get a hint on how to solve the puzzle at this point, but if the title of this section isn't enough of a give-away, then perhaps you should just skip ahead to the solution.

Solution

Vegetation Medication

Factoid

In what room of what world in Zork Nemesis can you find Prozork sitting on a bookshelf? Malveaux's bedroom, isn't it? Play the game through again and then let me know.

Toss the Prozork tablet into the snapdragon's mouth. It'll fall right to sleep. Then you can cut its head off with your sword. It won't actually die, as you see later.

Taken:	Used:
Snapdragon	**Prozork tablet**
	Sword

Preparations For a Later Puzzle

Now carry the snapdragon head to the back of the house and place it on the trampoline plant. You can hit the trampoline with the hammer you picked up from the emergency adventure case to make the snapdragon head bounce, but it won't bounce high enough to get it where you need it to go. Try casting Throck on the trampoline plant so that the coil tightens. Now walk to the front door of the house.

Used:
Snapdragon
Throck

You'll need to use this later on.

HARRY THE HOME SECURITY SYSTEM

A cursory click on the front door of the house demonstrates that unobstructed entrance into the Dungeon Master's Lair is not possible. The Dungeon Master installed Harry the home security system to protect his belongings. Harry is unwilling to listen to the Dungeon Master's request for entrance, given Dalboz's be-lamped condition.

As always, you can try to swashbuckle your way past the door, but as always, that would get you nowhere.

By now you've hopefully figured out what the Zimdor scroll is for. If not, put it in your item viewer and read it over and over again until it becomes apparent.

You're going to have to appeal to the security system's character flaws to get past it. You must listen to the Dungeon Master and deduce that weakness for yourself. Okay, you twisted my arm. Harry's a lousy drunk. It's his tragic flaw. Think about it.

Harry has a few bad habits that you can exploit.

Harry The Home Security System

Cast the Zimdor spell on your can of Mead. That triples its size, making it enough to get Harry drunk on. Now pour the can of Mead into the birdbath. If, by chance, you already poured the Mead into the birdbath, you can cast Zimdor on the birdbath and it will have the same effect.

Either way, Harry won't take the drink. He has to be put in the mood.

USED:
Cigar
Can of Mead
Zimdor

Place your cigar in the bowl to the left of Harry. Harry will indulge in a puff, blow half his door open, then take a drink from the birdbath, become immediately sloshed, and blow the other half open.

That'll take care of Harry... until tomorrow morning. Fortunately, you won't be around for that. You cad!

The Answering Machine

Step into the Dungeon Master's house, look around, read any books you find, and do whatever suits your fancy. This guy sat around doing nothing for a hundred years without magic, so you can imagine he's got a few back issues of "Wizard's Digest" stacked around the place.

When you're done, take a look at the phone near the window with the blinds drawn. Play through the messages on the machine.

Most of them are useless, but the message about the cocoa recipe is one very long hint. You might have to listen to the message a few times to get everything on the list she reads. You could write it all down. Or you could use this book where it's all written down for you.

You need the Flatheadia fudge (click on it with your sword), the glazed hungus lard, the moss of Mareilon, and the Quelbee honey. The first two items you'll find by looking around in this very room. The third, moss of Mareilon, you got back in the Flood Control Dam subway station.

You did get it, didn't you?

The last item, though, you do not have. You need to step back outside to get the Quelbee honey.

These are two of the many items you'll need to make the Dungeon Master's famous cocoa recipe.

You'll also want to pick up the jar of fireflies that's setting on the bookshelf next to the hungus lard, and the mug that's hanging from the tree. You'll need them both later.

Hint

QUELLING THE QUELBEES

Go outside the house and walk up to the Quelbee hive. The Dungeon Master gives you a fairly explicit hint about what to do. You need to ward them off with something that stinks. Now what in your inventory could possibly bear a stench? Have you dropped all of your items into the viewer?

P.S.—Using your sword here would not be advisable.

Don't screw around with the Quelbees. Do what you've got to do, and then get out.

Solution

QUELLING THE QUELBEES

TAKEN:	USED:
Quelbee honeycomb	**Hungus lard**
	Sword

Stick the hungus lard into the Quelbee nest and the Quelbees will flee in disgust. Remove the lard, then pull out your sword and hack a piece of honeycomb off.

THE FOOD PROCESSOR

To complete the food processor puzzle, all you have to do is put all the items you acquired in place. If you have the Flatheadia fudge, hungus lard, moss of Mareilon, Quelbee honey, jar of fireflies, and mug, then you're set. Drop all of those items into the food processor and in seconds you'll have a piping hot cup of cocoa.

TAKEN:	USED:
Yastard	**Flatheadia fudge**
	Hungus lard
	Moss of Mareilon
	Quelbee honey
	Jar of fireflies
	Mug

The aroma of cocoa jogs the Dungeon Master's memory; he suddenly recalls the Yastard spell and Gnustos it into your inventory. This is half of what you'll need to use the time tunnels.

Making the cocoa will use about half the items in your inventory.

ACT II: THE UNDERGROUND

The Walking Castle

Head over to the blinds on the far wall of the room and peek through them. You'll see the cute and lovable Walking Castle hopping around in the Dungeon Master's back yard. You need to get into the castle. You can't walk across the river because, as you can see, the golgatem spell doesn't work. You can't swim across the river because whatever prevented golgatem from working probably wouldn't take too kindly to you swimming around in there. You can't walk around the river because... because you can't.

Basically, you can't get to the castle. So you have to bring the castle to you. You can get some valuable information on how to do that by reading the book on the creatures of Zork that resides in this very room.

Solution

The Walking Castle

Cast Obidil on the castle while it's pacing in the distance to make it attracted to you. It will come running towards you, drawbridge wide open. Crawl through the blinds, walk across the drawbridge, and try not to think about what metaphorical significance this has for the already-aroused castle. And that's all I'm going to say about that.

Used:
Obidil

Inside the Castle

The only thing you need to do inside the castle, or the castle's innards as the case seems to be, is look closely at the beating heart/chandelier—cool, castle guts—and pull the scroll out from between its ventricles. It's the Narwile spell, and it's worth every one of the cold and sweaty flashbacks you're going to experience after reaching into a beating heart and pulling out a sheet of paper. You can now open time tunnels.

Taken:
Narwile

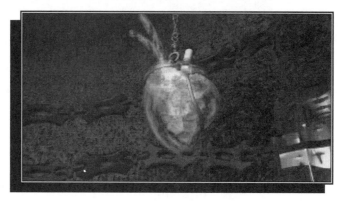

Reach inside the castle's heart and remove the Narwile Spell.

The Griff, the Spell, and the Wardrobe

Go back into the Dungeon Master's Lair and turn left. Walk through the doorway and you're in the Dungeon Master's bedroom. You'll come back to this in a minute, but first, turn to the wardrobe to the right of the doorway and open it up, anyway you like. Inside you'll find a glowing rift in space. That's no rift in the space-time continuum. That's a closed time tunnel, buddy. Cast Narwile on it to open it up.

USED:
Narwile
Yastard

You can't jump into it yourself. As the Dungeon Master explains, when beings of flesh pass through time tunnels, they typically suffer from side effects such as death, fatality, and loss of life. The only thing that can survive the journey is a Yastardized totem. Cast Yastard on the Griff to send him through.

You're about to enter the first of three time tunnel quests. Each quest is designed for a different totem. The totem that you just sent through isn't the right totem for this quest. However, it's the right totem to perform a minor task that you'll need done later on. So think of this as a prelude to the time tunnel quests.

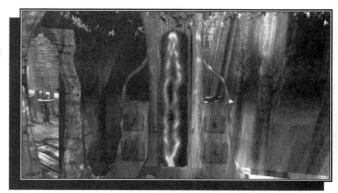

This is the first of three time tunnels that you will find in the underground.

Act II and 1/2:   Prelude to the
Time Tunnel Quests

The Griff is thrust through the time tunnel and ends up in an open field west of a white house. There's a small mailbox here.

WEST OF HOUSE

That's right, this is THE white house. No, not THAT white house. This is the white house from the first Zork text adventure (not Pennsylvania Avenue).

You'll notice that all of your spells and inventory are gone. That's because you are no longer you. You've only got a few things to do here as the Griff. You can explore later on when you come back as the Brog.

TAKEN:	USED:
Envelope	**Envelope**
Glorf	

Take a closer look at the mailbox in front of you. Open it up and take out the envelope inside. Whatever you put in this enve-

The famed white house of Zork.

lope will be mailed to you in the afterlife. It may not seem like the most useful of things, but what you want to put inside it is the Glorf spell scroll that's on the side of the house. It allows you to untie knots. Because the mailbox is so high up (compared to the rather short Brog), you can only get to it with the Griff's flight capabilities.

Get the scroll, stuff it into the envelope in your inventory, stick the envelope back into the mailbox, and don't forget to raise the flag on the side.

That's it. Now jump back through the time tunnel.

A Brief Note on the Space-Time Continuum

To ease any confusion about the effects of changing the past, here's a quick explanation.

Changing the past changes the present. If you go back to the past and change something, it will have changed in that way when you return to the present. But if you go back into the past again after changing it once, everything in the past resets to the way that it was before you changed it, and you then have to change it again for it to be that way when you get back. Or you could change it a different way if you weren't happy with the way that you changed it the first time. This is good, because if you really screw things up, you can always go back and fix them.

Factoid

I had to go ahead and explain the time travel dynamics, out of respect for one of the Designers on this project. Matt Harding was initially really distressed over several sub points of the Quendoran Space-Time Continuum. Micheal Douglas, the Lead Programmer, responded "Oh for the days when I was so young and idealistic about time travel," and the issue was never mentioned again.

OUT OF THE CLOSET

You pop back out of the wardrobe and retake control of your body. You now have all of your spells and inventory back.

You're now free to look around the Dungeon Master's bedroom. Read the journal on his bed to learn more about time tunnels and the man that was Dalboz. When you're done, pick up the torn piece of scroll on the windowsill and stand in front of the mirror.

The scroll piece that you're holding is half of the Snavig scroll. You've got a long way to go until it's in your spell book.

Step through the mirror and you'll find yourself standing in a mirror image of the room you just left. It's the mirror room. Everything in this room is exactly like it is in the other room, except flipped. Even your controls are flipped.

Step up to the windowsill and take the scroll piece that's lying there. Look at it in your inventory and you'll discover that it's not a flipped version of the piece in the

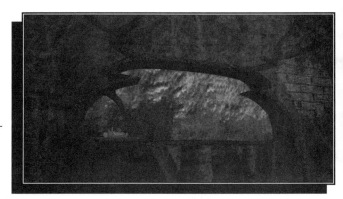

To reassemble the Snavig scroll you need to get both halves to face the right direction at the same time.

bedroom, but rather the other half of the same scroll. Unfortunately, it's facing the wrong way. But if you look at the first piece that you picked up, you'll find that it's facing the right way.

TAKEN:
"GIV-" scroll piece
"-ANS" scroll piece

If you were to walk through the mirror again and go back to the regular bedroom, the first piece would go back to facing the wrong way, but the piece from the mirror room would be right.

THE SNAVIG PUZZLE

The problem lies in getting both pieces to face in the proper direction at the same time. No matter how many times you walk back and forth, you're never going to get both pieces the way you want them unless you figure out a way to get around the problem.

The Snapdragon helps you smuggle part of the Snavig scroll out through a side route.

Solution

THE SNAVIG PUZZLE

Put the first scroll piece that you found in the regular bedroom (the one that said "GIV-") and place it on the windowsill of the mirror room. Now walk all the way outside and around to the back of the house where the trampoline plant is still sitting with the snapdragon on it. The trampoline plant is directly underneath the mirror room windowsill. Get it?

The last time you were here, you cast Throck on the trampoline plant to make its coil tighten. Now whack the trampoline plant with the hammer that you picked up in the adventure case to make the snapdragon head bounce up to the windowsill. It grabs the scroll piece and leaps back down.

Take the scroll piece out of the snapdragon's mouth. If you did things right, the "-ANS" scroll piece that you picked up in the mirror room should be facing the right direction, and so should the "GIV-" that you got in the bedroom. Combining the two gives you a not-quite-valid version of the Snavig spell. You still have to run it through the Spell Checker.

Taken:	Used
Ripped Snavig scroll	**Snapdragon**
	Hammer
	"GIV-" scroll piece
	"-ANS" scroll piece

One Last Visit to GUE Tech

Go to the Teleportation Station behind the Dungeon Master's house and jump to the Spell Labs. Walk to the Spell Checker and run the Snavig scroll through the machine. When it comes out it will be ready to Gnusto into your spell book.

Once that's done, walk back across the bridge and teleport to Hades.

Hades isn't where you want to be yet, but it's the nearest jump station to the Flood Control Dam. The Flood Control Dam is where you want to be, so go to the subway map, select it, and ride the subway there.

Taken:	Used:
Snavig	**Ripped Snavig scroll**

One Last Visit to Flood Control Dam #3

Now that you have money, you can step up to the zorkmid press and put a coin in the machine. When it comes out, it will have been pressed into a letter opener. Hmm, a letter opener…

Anyway, go to the subway map and ride it back to Hades. When you're there, walk through the subway stop to the shore where the Hades Shuttle Service Courtesy Phone is.

The zorkmid press supplies you with an indescribably valuable adventuring tool.

Taken:	Used:
Letter opener	**Zorkmid**

Hades Courtesy Phone Puzzle

At long last you're ready to cross the River Styx. To do this, you'll need to solve the most dastardly and convoluted puzzle in the entire game. The makers of ZGI force you, the player, to not just visit Hell, but experience it for yourself—in the form of a computerized touch-tone phone operator that just doesn't seem to give a damn about whether or not you understand a word she's saying. If you listen carefully, you will be able to simply follow her maddening directions,

The Hades Phone Operator can supply endless hours of suffering and torment.

and emerge victorious. Especially if you take good notes. If you aren't the patient, methodical type, think like a wizard. Because how many patient, methodical wizards do you know?

HADES COURTESY PHONE PUZZLE

If this were a precise, detailed strategy guide, it would give you a long list of everything the Hades phone voice says and all the touch-tone options it presents. It would tell you all the buttons to press and exactly why you're pressing them so that when you completed the puzzle, you would feel victorious and fulfilled.

But that would deprive you all of the pleasure of the humor, the sadism, the thrill that is the Hades Phone Puzzle. So all this strategy guide tells you is that the fastest, easiest, and—doggone it—the best way to solve this puzzle is to cast the Kendall spell on it to clear away all the mumbo jumbo. Once you do that, just press the button that the voice on the phone tells you to. The shuttle comes, the puzzle is over, and you have saved yourself a lot of time.

> USED:
>
> **2 zorkmids**
>
> **Kendall**

Now walk up to the oarsman. He'll ask you for two zorkmids to get across. Pull them out of your coin sack one at a time and give them to him.

HADES POSTAL SERVICE PUZZLE

Step off the shuttle and you'll see a gateway in the distance with a strange creature guarding it. Ignore the creature for now and walk up to the gate.

Look at the mailbox to the left of the gate. Open it up and take the envelope out. It's the letter you sent to yourself from outside the white house. But alas, it's sealed. And what unholy force could possibly break such a seal as this?

A pleasant surprise could be waiting for you inside this mailbox.

HADES POSTAL SERVICE PUZZLE

Open the envelope with your letter opener. No, it's not junk mail. You get the Glorf spell.

TAKEΠ:	USED:
Glorf	**Letter**
Opener	

GETTING PAST THE HADES BEAST

All right, you're all clear to turn your attention to the two-headed beast that's guarding the entrance to Hades. He is, of course, none to willing to let you by.

You can attack him with your sword, you can dazzle him with your letter opener, you can flog him with your map. Nothing works. He's not interested, he's not letting you by, and the longer you bug him, the closer he'll get to biting your head off.

Once again, he's not letting YOU by. That's YOU, being the Adventurer that YOU are, and having no business in a place such as Hades, which is specifically reserved for those who are dead.

Solution

GETTING PAST THE HADES BEAST

In case that wasn't clear enough, you have to approach him as someone else. To do that, you have to cast the Snavig spell. And who's nearby to cast the spell on?

Walk up to the oarsman and cast Snavig on him. Now walk up to the two-headed Hades beast as the oarsman (and do it fast, you have only a limited amount of time). He'll think you're going on your lunch break and

The Hades Beast is under strict instructions not to let any non-Hades personnel by.

let you by. But you've got to punch out first, which means you have to know who you are. Hopefully, you were paying attention earlier, and know that the oarsman's

USED:
Snavig

name is Charon. If not, you hopefully just read the last sentence. Either way, choose the card on the bottom left that's marked "Charon."

The gates open and you can walk through.

BEYOND THE GATES OF HADES

Past the gates, you'll notice another time tunnel. Before entering, turn around and pick up the totem that's lying on the ground. It's the Brog. He's short and stupid, but incredibly strong. Watch the video clip that explains how he got totemized, and then put him in that

handy dandy rucksack you call an inventory. You'll use him later.

TAKEN:	USED:
Brog totem	*Narwile*
	Yastard

Anyway, open the time tunnel with the Narwile spell and cast Yastard on the Griff to toss him through again. This is the quest that the Griff actually belongs in.

ACT ÏÏ AND 3/4:   THE TÏME TUNNEL QUESTS

You have just embarked on your first time tunnel quest. You're now well on your way to completing the game.

The Dragon Archipelago

You arrive as the Griff on a small green island with a steep incline. It shouldn't take you long to figure out that this cluster of islands is actually a giant, sleeping dragon. And that hot spring in the distance is actually smoke pouring out of the dragon's nostrils.

This is the same dragon that, a century ago, swallowed the ship carrying the Coconut of Quendor. You need to get that coconut back and return it to the present. To do that, you need to get inside the dragon's mouth. And to do that, you need to get his head out of the water.

You can't quite clear the distance to the hands or the head, but you can use the Griff's short-range flight capability to hop over to the other foot. Of course, swimming is out of the question, as the water is filled with deadly water-grues that will devour you on site.

Taken:

Inflatable sea captain

Inflatable boat

Air pump

At the other foot, turn to the dragon's toes and pull the one on the far right. When you turn back around, the dragon's stomach will have risen to the surface. It's not your place to ask why. That's just the way dragon bodies work. You can now fly to the stomach, and from there, the dragon's hands and head.

Fly to the dragon's right hand and pull the air pump from the skeleton's hands. In case you're wondering why a perfectly preserved skeleton is holding an air pump while standing on one knee in the palm of a dragon's hand... stop it, it's not worth the effort.

Anyway, fly back to the stomach and pull the inflatable boat and the inflatable sea captain out of the chest.

The Giant Watchdragon of the Great Sea is guarding one of the treasures.

Hint

"What Do You Do With an Inflatable Sailor?"

You now have an inflatable boat, an inflatable sea captain, and an air pump to inflate them with. It would seem pretty natural to inflate them at this point, wouldn't it? But where would that get you? You don't need a boat, cause you can fly. And aside from pulling the sea captain's cord and listening to him talk, he's not good for much either.

This is how the dragon breathes underwater.

Perhaps they could somehow be useful in solving the bigger problem that you face in this area. What was that again?

Solution

"What Do You Do With an Inflatable Sailor?"

Used:
Air pump
Inflatable sea captain
Inflatable boat

Fly up to the dragon's head, stick the un-inflated sea captain into one nostril and the un-inflated boat into the other. Inflate them both while they're in the nostrils. When both nostrils are plugged, the dragon lifts its head out of the water, allowing you to fly inside.

Heisting the Coconut

Hovering inside the dragon's mouth is, needless to say, not an entirely pleasant experience for the Griff. He would like to get through with this quest as soon as possible, and would be happy to just grab the coconut sitting in front of him and fly out. However, every time he does that, the dragon's mouth slams shut.

The dragon doesn't seem to mind that you've flown into its mouth, but it draws the line at stealing the coconut. You'll have to be more clever.

You soon discover that you're not alone inside the dragon. A man named Sneffle is living down in the throat. He's only important for the rope that he tosses up to you, so you can pretty much ignore him. Just take the rope from him and let him fall to his death.

The other thing you're going to need is the chipped-off piece of one of the dragon's teeth. Pick that up as well.

Also, make sure you look up in the nostrils at the boat and the sea captain. They're still there.

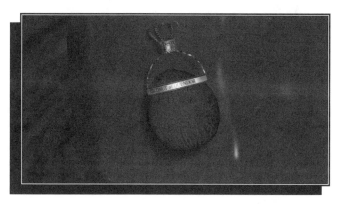

Here dangles the Coconut of Quendor.

Here are a couple possible solutions that won't work:

Throwing the coconut down the dragon's throat dead-ends you, and you'll have to jump through the time tunnel then back in again in order to reset it. Popping either of the inflatables only causes the dragon's head to go back down.

You now have everything you need to get the coconut out of the mouth.

Heisting the Coconut

Alrighty, the first thing you need to do is look in the nostril with the inflatable boat in it. There's a pouch on the boat that you can stick the coconut into. Put it in there.

Now fly outside the mouth (which you can do safely as long as you're not holding the coconut) and tie the boat to the sea captain's leg so that they're connected on the outside.

Fly back into the mouth, look into the nostril with the sea captain in it, and pop it with the piece of the dragon's tooth. It shoots out the nose and whizzes around in the air for a few seconds with the inflatable boat in tow before crashing into the water and sinking.

The boat, however, is still inflated, and still has the Coconut of Quendor resting in its pouch. Hurry out of the mouth because, with his nose clear, the dragon is submerging.

You can find the boat floating near the stomach. Remove the coconut and the very same walking castle that you encountered in the Dungeon Master's Lair bursts through the surface with its drawbridge open.

Fly into the walking castle and place the coconut down on the pedestal. Which pedestal, you ask? Well, it would have to be the only one that gives you a hot spot, wouldn't it?

Once that's done, a time tunnel opens up inside the castle and you can jump through to return to the gates of Hades in the present day, the coconut safely stored away for later.

Taken:	Used:
Rope	**Rope**
Shard of dragon's tooth	**Shard of dragon's tooth**
Coconut of Quendor	

To Hades and Back

After a brief stay at an island getaway in the Great Sea, you have returned to the gates of Hades, where you left off. Now you need to get back across the River Styx to continue your quest.

Had you approached Charon, the oarsman, about getting back across before passing through the gates, he would have taken pity on you and given you a free ride. However, you have now been through the gates, and are thus bound to the strictest of laws by which Charon must abide; absolutely no one is allowed back from Hades once they've passed through the gates.

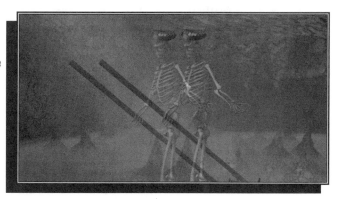

Once you've passed through the gates, getting back from Hades isn't quite so easy.

Doh! Now what are you going to do?

To Hades and Back

To get back from Hades, you must use the same trick that got you in. Cast Snavig, but this time cast it on the Hades beast instead of Charon. When you walk up to Charon as the Hades beast, he'll gladly take you across the river without thinking twice about it... Get it? Twice? Two heads?

Anyway, once you've gotten across, step up to the Teleportation Station nearby and jump to the Dungeon Master's Lair.

<table>
<tr><td>USED:
Snavig</td><td>*Walk back into the Dungeon Master's bedroom and open the wardrobe. Cast Narwile to open it up, but this time, cast Yastard on your new Brog totem instead of the Griff.*</td></tr>
</table>

THE BROG QUEST

⊙UTSIDE THE WHITE HOUSE AGAIN

You're back at the white house, but this time you're the Brog. Turn around and walk to the stone barrow in the distance. This is the hidden area that appeared at the end of *Zork I*. Beyond this door lies the area from *Zork II*. But you can't go there in this game. In fact, all you can do here is pull the flickering and the bickering torches off of their torch-holders. Do that.

<table>
<tr><td>TAKEN:
Flickering torch
Bickering torch
Wooden board</td></tr>
</table>

You'll need these torches in a minute when you descend into the pitch black grue breeding ground.

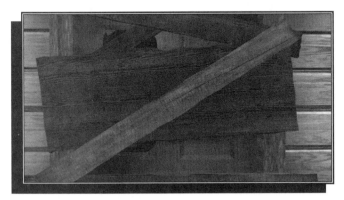

As the Brog, you can pull the boards off the front door of the house.

Now turn around and head back to the house. Walk to the boarded-up front door and use your tremendous strength to pull the boards off. You automatically keep one of them and put it in your inventory. Climb through the hole in the door and walk into the darkness.

HEY, WHAT HAPPENED TO THE INSIDE OF THE HOUSE?

FACTOID

"The grue is a sinister, lurking presence in the dark places of the earth. Its favorite diet is Adventurers, but its insatiable appetite is tempered by its fear of light. No grue has ever been seen by the light of day, and few have survived its fearsome jaws to tell the tale."

Excerpted from Zork I

You're now standing inside the house. Or at least, where the house should be. You have actually just passed through a weird space anomaly that has put you at the entrance to a grue breeding ground. Ignore the nearby campfire for now and head down the stairs to the breeding ground.

YOU CAN'T MAKE AN OMELETTE...

At the bottom of the stairs you'll find a pile of rocks, a pile of eggs, and a cliff edge. Way off in the distance, you can see a strange-looking contraption that you sense has some relevance to your quest.

You need to get across the breeding ground to the strange contraption, but if you go, the torches douse themselves in fear. You obviously can't just get across—you need to do something first.

Take a look at the stalactites. There's a tiny shaft of light creeping through one of them. If you were to chip away at the shaft, it might grow big enough to illuminate the room.

The pile of rocks might help. But the Brog chomps them down every time you click on them.

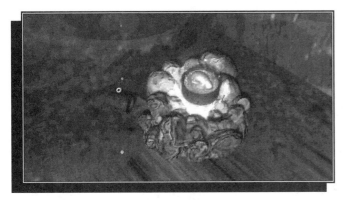

Go over to the other pile and take an egg. The Brog isn't as interested in those. You can throw one of the eggs at the stalactites, but it'll just crack and make the grues lurking in the room even more angry.

So what do you do with it?

A hard-boiled egg does much more damage when thrown than a normal egg.

You Can't Make an Omelette...

Remember the campfire up at the top of the stairs? Run back up to it and drop the egg into the can of water. Light the fire with your flickering torch and the egg hard-boils. You now have a much more useful item to throw.

Taken:	Used:
Egg	**Hard Boiled Egg**
	Flickering torch

Go back to the cliff edge and throw the hard-boiled egg at the stalactites. They break off and clear a path to the contraption.

The Strange-Looking Contraption

You're now standing in front of a strange contraption that's decorated with some elaborate chess puzzle, à la "The 7th Guest." The Skull of Yoruk is inside at

the top, but it's locked inside of a steel ball. You can move the chess pieces on the three boards, but the Brog doesn't seem to quite get what's going on. This puzzle appears to be beyond his, yours, and our comprehension.

You must solve this baffling brain-teaser in order to take the Skull of Yoruk.

THE STRANGE-LOOKING CONTRAPTION

Take the board that you picked up earlier and smash the heck out of that contraption, then pull the skull out of its confines. That's how a Brog plays "7th Guest," too.

The castle arrives outside the house as soon as you pick up the Skull of Yoruk. Walk into the castle and put the skull on its pedestal.

TAKEN:	USED:
Skull of Yoruk	**Wooden board**

A time tunnel opens up. Jump through the time tunnel and return to the Dungeon Master's bedroom in time to see Jack ratting on you to the Grand Inquisitor. Looks like the GI is on to you.

THE WONDERS OF GLORF

TAKEN:	USED:
Rope	**Glorf**

You're finished with the Dungeon Master's Lair, so head out. You can either walk back to the underground crossroads or use the teleporter. It takes about the same amount of time. From the crossroads, walk over to the dragon staircase and ride it back up to the well bottom.

Remember that rope that you couldn't untie before? Now you can untie it magically with your Glorf spell.

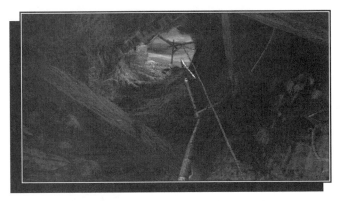

This is where you use the handy dandy untie rope spell.

One Last Subway Ride

You're almost finished with the underground. There's just one last area to explore. It's time to go inside the belly of the beast—the Inquisition headquarters at the old Steppinthrax Monastery.

Head back down the dragon stairs, walk through the underground crossroads to the subway, select the monastery from the subway map, and ride it to your destination.

Fun with Grates

The only thing to do in the monastery subway stop is walk over to the crumbled staircase and look up. There's a grate hanging open in the ceiling. That's how you're going to enter the monastery. But how are you gonna lift yourself up there?

Two of your items can combine to help you climb through the grate.

That rope you just picked up could be useful, but it won't stay up there if you just throw it. You need to get one end of it stuck up there.

Fun With Grates

Tie the rope to the sword by going into your inventory, putting the sword in the close-up viewer, then clicking on it with the rope. Throw the combined object up through the grate. The sword hangs over either side of the hole, allowing you to climb the rope and pull yourself up into the totemizer room.

USED:
Sword
Rope

The Dreaded Totemizer Machine

You climb the rope and end up in the Inquisition's totemization room. Directly in front of you is the dreaded totemizer machine. Doesn't the sight of that thing just fill you with dread? Can't you hear the anthem to the Death Star echoing in your ears? In a minute, you're going to have to ride through it. It's the only way you can get to the elusive portal of your next treasure quest. But first you must make a number of careful preparations, my friend. Set the machine to suit your adventuring needs. Make sure the machine is set to take you where you want to go—and not to do any permanent damage.

The Dreaded Totemizer Machine.

THE DREADED TOTEMIZER MACHINE

Before you do anything else, make sure you turn off the Perma-Seal on the totemizer machine. It's a small container on the top of the machine with a pink light next to it. If you turn the Perma-Seal off, the totemizer will return you to your normal size once you finish riding through it. If you leave it on, you will spend the rest of eternity trapped inside the tiny steel case. To turn it off, turn the wheel to shut the valve with the green light on it. When the light is off, so is the Perma-Seal.

There's a panel nearby with a list of five possible destinations. The "Straight to Hell" is a safe but useless choice that you've already been to.

"The Airless Surface of Murz" is a very cool little Easter egg. It's a set of actual photographs from the recent Sojourner mission to Mars that have been turned into a panoramic surround. Unfortunately, the "Airless" part should key you in that going there will result in death.

The "Newark, New Jersey" option is a pleasant alternative to finishing the game. If you so choose to be dumped there, you will live out the rest of your life in moderately un-fulfilled, but otherwise sublime happiness. If you're interested in finishing the game, however, then just ignore it.

The option that you want is the one labeled "To Hall of Inquisition." That takes you to the Monastery Exhibit Hall, which is where you want to be.

Once you've turned off the Perma-Seal and selected "To Hall of Inquisition" as your destination, you can safely hop inside the machine by pulling the lever to the left of the entrance door.

Spin the wheel on the right to turn off the Perma-Seal.

The "Perils of Magic" Exhibit

After a wacky and fun-filled ride through the totemizer machine (it always reminds me of that part of *Charlie and the Chocolate Factory* where Willy Wonka takes you on the boat and you see the colors and the bugs, and then the whole thing just stops) you pop out in a large bin in the corner of the Monastery Exhibit Hall. This is where the public comes to see that magic stunk and that they should be content with their miserable lives, because they would be much more miserable if wizards and alchemists were still running around. By and large, this isn't true. But the Grand Inquisitor has selected a few choice McNuggets of Zork history to exploit as evidence of his claim.

Shortly after arriving, you will un-perma-seal and return to your normal size. Happy? Immediately after this happens, you hear a woman's voice hollering nearby. If you look back into the display bin you'll see another totem sitting in there. It's Lucy Flathead, that notorious babe of a telepath, figure(flat)head of the magic rebellion, and sole survivor of the once-powerful Flathead line. Watch the video on her unfortunate arrest and totemization and she will appear as the last addition to your totem collection.

> **Taken:**
> ***Lucy totem***

Take a look at the four exhibits, but pay particular attention to the one about time tunnels. When you press the button, you see the little metal man hammering the last board over a time tunnel. Set the lever to its fastest speed, then press the button again. The little man will hammer frantically until the hammer breaks and snaps off. Don't you just hate it when that happens?

What you need to do now is put something else in the little man's hands that will break the wooden boards off. You can try the other little hammer that you picked up from the Emergency Adventure case, but that isn't what you need.

This diorama shows an Inquisition Guard sealing off one of the time tunnels.

THE TELEGRAPH MACHINE

There are doors on either end of the room. One of them takes you back to the totemization room and then locks behind you. Don't go through that one. Go to the door on the far end of the room, past the time tunnel diorama, and walk outside.

This is how messages get sent to the Inquisition Guards.

Walk to the gate and turn to your left. You'll see a strange metal cylinder. Open it up and look inside. There are three hammers banging out messages in the special Inquisition code. This is an Inquisition telegraph machine. If you look on the gate to your right, you'll see a bunch of different messages that can be sent. Most of them will result in amusing death. But one of them will let all of the Inquisition guards off work early tonight, and result in no fatal side effects for you. You need to remove one of the telegraph hammers, and the one to remove is the one that will result in that message being sent.

It's confusing, but it ultimately doesn't really matter anyway. All you need to do is go into the machine, pull out the middle hammer, then step away and walk back to the time tunnel diorama. That's it.

> **TAKEN:**
> *Telegraph hammer*

BACK AT THE DIORAMA

> **USED:**
> *Telegraph Hammer*
> *Narwile*
> *Yastard*
> *Lucy totem*

Back at the diorama, slap the telegraph hammer into the little man's hands, then turn him on at full speed again. He now wields with the might needed to smash through the boards. He does so, revealing that there actually is a genuine time tunnel inside the display. Cast Narwile on it to open it up, as usual. Then cast Yastard on the Lucy totem to toss her in and begin her quest.

The Lucy Quest

Old Port Foozle

The time tunnel drops you off back in Port Foozle, where you started out the game. However, you're no longer in the present day. You are in the year 931 GUE, well over 100 years back in time. Granted, things haven't changed very much, but one thing that has changed is Antharia Jack's Pawn Shack. In this day and age it's a speakeasy casino. Walk up to the door and knock.

The big, burly casino bouncer Floyd sees you, the sultry Lucy Flathead—are you feeling sultry right now?—and in an all-too-creepy manner, opens the door to let you in. You suspect that if you were, say, the Brog or the Griff, you most certainly would not get the same treatment.

> **Used:**
> ***Feminine Wiles Aplenty***

This is old Port Foozle, long before the Inquisitor's Dark Reign.

APINE'S QUANDARY

You're now inside the casino. It is surprisingly empty. In fact, there aren't really many games to play. There's a Pachinko machine in back, but it's about as engaging as Pachinko is in real life.

There's a dart board, but there aren't any darts. Basically, the room is completely barren with the exception of a strange playing card puzzle that someone left unfinished on one of the tables. There's a plaque on the top of the board labeled "Apine's Quandary." There are four slots underneath, separated by a division symbol, a subtraction symbol, and an equal sign. At the front of the table are four cards with dots marking the value of each card, from 1 through 4. You can pick up all four cards.

The obvious thing to do here—for anyone with even the vaguest recollection of basic mathematics—is to place the cards in the slots to make the equation correct. But try as you might, you can't find a single arrangement that makes sense. You put all four cards down, the reader passes over it, then lights up and tells you that the equation doesn't work.

You need to find some way to beat it. Do not rule cheating out as a method.

Apine's Quandary isn't as easy as it looks. In fact, it's pretty much impossible without cheating.

Semi Final Solution

Apine's Quandary

Do you hear that buzzing noise in the distance? Walk around the room and you'll hear it getting closer and farther away. If you follow the noise across the room, you'll find a bug buzzing around a lamp on one of the walls. It swirls around for a few seconds, then stops and sits, then continues buzzing wildly for another few seconds.

> **Taken:**
>
> **Cards**
>
> **Card with dead bug on it**

You can smack it with any one of your four cards. Smack it with the 4 card, and the bug splatters right in the middle. If you look at it in your close-up viewer, the card now resembles a 5 card. Hmm... How could that be helpful?

If, by chance, you opt to smack it with a different card, you will make that card appear to be one number higher. But that doesn't matter. You want the bug's carcass on the 4 card, so put the 4 in your object viewer and click on it with whichever of the other cards you mistakenly crushed it with.

Once that's done, go back to Apine's Quandary and see if you can solve the equation now.

Final Solution

Apine's Quandary

The equation should be 5 / 1 - 3 = 2, or it could also be 5 / 1 - 2 = 3. Either one works. Once completed, Floyd the Bouncer appears and congratulates you. You are then invited into the back room to play with a real high-roller.

> **Used:**
>
> **Card with dead bug on it**

Jack's Back

And guess who that high-roller is? It's Antharia Jack. He's over a century younger than he was at the beginning of the game, although you wouldn't know it to look at him. Jack's one of those guys who always looks about 35. Guess it's that Macrobiotic diet. And the cigars.

Anyway, Jack has challenged you to a game of Strip Grue, Fire, Water. It would be a very good idea to take him up on that offer, as he is secretly harboring the elusive Cube of Foundation that you've been searching for. And, knowing Jack, it's probably in his shorts.

Sit down at the table and get ready to play.

How to Win at Strip Grue, Fire, Water

The rules to Strip Grue, Fire, Water are very simple. In fact, they're identical to the rules for Rocks, Paper, Scissors, with the exception that when you lose a round, you have to take off an item of clothing. Other than that, it's just as Floyd says: grue drinks water, water puts out fire, fire scares grue.

Jack's strategy at Strip "Grue, Fire, Water" is a little transparent.

There are three buttons in front of you. One has a picture of fire on it, another has a picture of water, and the third bears an image of a grue (shrouded in total darkness). You pick one of the buttons to push, and Jack picks one as well. The machine reads the two and indicates a win, a loss, or a tie.

You can go ahead and play the game, but as you play you may find it rather irritating that whether or not you win or lose is completely random. Wouldn't it be nice to have some way of bettering your odds? It sure would...

How to Win at Strip Grue, Fire, Water

Lucy's a telepath, remember? Click on Jack's silhouette on the curtain to read his mind. He tells you which button he's about to push, and you'll have a few seconds to deduce which one will beat him.

Each time you win, Jack takes off another garment. First comes his shirt, then his undershirt, then his pants, then his precious hat, and finally it's down to just his underwear. If you win that round, poor old Jack will get embarrassed and offer you the Cube that he found instead.

Take the cube and run into the walking castle that has conveniently reappeared right outside the casino. Put the cube on the last pedestal, then jump back through the time tunnel when it appears.

Taken:	Used:
Cube of Foundation	**Telepathic abilities**
Jack's manhood	**Shame**

That's all there is to it. You're done with the three treasure quests.

Unfortunately...

Returning from your last quest results in your being immediately apprehended by the Grand Inquisitor and thrown into the Inquisition jail to await totemization. Bummer.

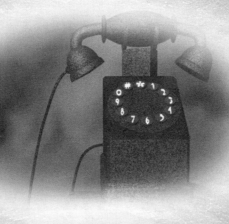

Aст iii

BREAKING OUT OF JAIL

You have been thrown in jail by the Grand Inquisitor, and are helpless while he unveils his diabolical new creation, Inquizivision, upon the populace at the Flathead Mesa. Try to say that twenty times... fast. And then say Vitameatavegimin.

Well, maybe you're not entirely helpless. Looking in your inventory, you aren't too surprised to find that... Hey! The guards have stripped you of your inventory. However, they did overlook the letter opener that you picked up at the Flood Control Dam. Perhaps it could still serve another purpose. Hmmm.

You hear an echoing voice nearby. It's grating. No—it's coming from the grate. It's Antharia Jack. He's stuck in here, too. Hmmm.

He talks to you for a while, rambling on about time tunnels and the Grand Inquisitor. He's crying. He thinks you're crying—what he says doesn't matter so much as what he does in a gesture of camaraderie. He tosses down a scroll to blow your nose with. Lo and behold, it's the Lexdom scroll; handy for creating locks in doors that don't already have them. An obscure spell indeed, but one that could prove eerily useful in your current situation. Since you don't have your spell book on you, you can't Gnusto it in, and thus, can only use it once. But who cares? You'll only need it once.

Walk over to the cell door and cast Lexdom on it. A lock drills itself into the door, and when you peek through it you see a key on the other side.

Now take a step back and look around the room. There's a notice on the wall telling you about what's going to happen to you. It can be ripped down. Take it and put it in your inventory.

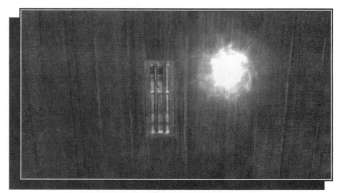

Think before you click. You need to get the key on your side of the door.

You now have everything you need to get out of the cell. Be careful, though. This part is easy to screw up.

BREAKING OUT OF JAIL

Poking the key out of the keyhole with your letter opener dead-ends you if you fail to make the proper preparations. So before you do it, slide the totemization notice under the door.

Pushing the key with the letter opener now causes it to fall on the notice, which you can then slide back under the door.

Take the key off the notice and put it into the lock on your side. The key turns and the door opens up.

Now all you have to do is get all your stuff and you'll be ready to head for the Flathead Mesa.

TAKEN:	USED:
Lexdom	**Lexdom**
Notice	**Notice**
Key	**Key**
	Letter Opener

GETTING YOUR STUFF BACK

You walk out of your cell and into the cell block. Unfortunately, you're stuck there. If you turn around the corner, you'll find a security system including a monitor. On the screen, by some cosmic coincidence, you see your good friend Antharia Jack. Take notice of the cell block number listed at the top of the screen.

Now step back and look at the map nearby. If you look at the cell block that the security

FACTOID

This puzzle is a blatant rip-off of a puzzle in Zork II, but heck, it's still a good puzzle.

monitor indicated Jack was in, and note where you are and the state of the stuff in the view, you'll find that Jack is in cell 31-AB.

There's a panel next to the monitors. The panel has a cell number entry pad and a button to open the door of that cell. Enter the exact numbers and letters that indicate Jack's cell and press the button to open it up.

Jack is then freed from his cell. He sneaks covertly around the jail and runs to pick up your inventory on the way to meet you outside your cell. Seconds after he arrives, the walking castle appears once again to carry you to the Flathead Mesa.

Jack is stuck in his cell, awaiting totemization.

Reversing Your Spells

You step out onto the back side of Flathead Mesa in the midst of the Grand Inquisitor's speech. It looks like the GI is about to launch Inquizivision once and for all.

Mid speech, you are greeted by the Enchantress Y'Gael, who brings you yet another gift. This one is the Booznik spell, which reverses all the other spells in your spell book.

Taken:	Used:
Booznik	**Booznik**
Skull	
Coconut	
Cube	

Take the scroll and cast it on your spell book, then watch as each one of your spells is flipped. This is the last new item that you will pick up in the game. You're almost there.

Before proceeding to the tower, head back to the castle and retrieve the Skull, Coconut, and Cube.

Act iii

GETTING PAST THE TENT

You walk past the screen that Y'Gael just appeared on and check out the tower in the distance. It's probably the same tower that Y'Gael was talking about.

This would all be good and fine were it not for the tent full of Inquisition guards blocking your path. If you walk by it, the guards inside will see you and smite liberally. Smitation will, as Wartle says, be in order.

You need to trap them inside the tent. Have you looked at your new spell book?

You'll need one of your new spells to get past this tent.

GETTING PAST THE TENT—SOLUTION

USED:
Vorzer

Cast the Vorzer spell. It's the reversed version of Rezrov. The door seals and you can safely walk by.

Unseen Obstacle

You approach the tower, but the Dungeon Master is very uneasy about moving further. He senses some unseen obstacle in front of you. You notice random patterns of electric sparks.

You need to find out what's blocking your path. Have you looked at your new spell book?

It may look clear, but something is still blocking your path.

Unseen Obstacle

USED:
Margi
Sword

Cast the Margi spell. It's the reversed version of Igram. (Not to mention my first name.) An invisible electric fence appears in purple. You can deactivate it by looking to the side where the socket is and unplugging it. All you have to do then is cut a hole in it with your sword and walk through.

PLACING THE ARTIFACTS

In order to bind high, middle, and deep together, returning magic to the land, you must place each of the three artifacts in the correct place along the tower.

The Skull of Yoruk, being the receptacle of deep magic, goes in the glass dome at the bottom. Open the dome, place the skull inside, shut it, then climb up the tower.

The Cube of Foundation, being the container for middle magic, goes in the nook halfway up the tower.

The Coconut of Quendor, being the symbol for high magic, goes in one of the balls of the wind gauge thingy at the top of the tower. Unfortunately, when you stick it inside, the wind gauge thingy becomes unbalanced. The Dungeon Master instructs you to hang his lantern on the opposite side to balance it out.

This is it. You're moments away from returning magic to Zork—or falling to your death.

Binding the Energies of Magic

The Dungeon Master pretty much takes the reins from here. He tells you to cast the Maxov spell to bind the energies of the different magics. Sure enough, the Voxam spell that you started the game with finally has a purpose. Try casting the spell.

Cut the wire to shut the Grand Inquisitor up—and the stage is set for victory!

Upon casting it, you learn from the Dungeon Master that the Grand Inquisitor's babbling is clouding the spell's effect. You need to shut him up.

There's a wire dangling just above you. Cut it with your sword. Right around then, Antharia Jack kicks in with his part of the plan, which was to create a distraction. To your

153

dismay, you find that his clever distraction was to point your presence out to the Grand Inquisitor himself in the middle of his speech. The Grand Inquisitor immediately comes chasing after you.

You have only a few seconds to cast Maxov again before the Grand Inquisitor climbs the tower and stops you. Hurry!

Once you cast the spell, the magics bind, a wave of energy shoots out across the landscape, the totems return to their original form, and magic returns to Zork.

Congratulations, you've won the game. You think you're hot? Now try it on the medium skill level.

Kidding.

Chapter V:
Magic in Zork
Grand Inquisitor

Universal Magic—Unauthorized and Banned.
For Officers of the Inquisition Only

This background report was recovered from a file cabinet full of partially-burnt dossiers in Chief Undersecretary Wartle's cubicle at Steppinthrax Monastery. The author is unknown.

Universal Magic

Though the Wizards, Enchanters, Invokers, Diviners, Mages, Necromancers, Sorcerers and Dungeon Masters of the Great Underground Empire have long been Unionized, they have remarkably little control over the course of Magic in Zork. That is to say, though Thaumaturgy is regulated, Enchanters are licensed, and Spells are copyrighted, and Hyperbolic Incantation Concentrators patented, painted and perfumed—the actual sources of power within the Zork Magical Landscape have been left largely unexcavated.

And in a Magical Universe, it is the Universe itself that ultimately possesses the greater part of the magic. So it is in the GUE; where the Stuff of Magic is wild and natural, not to mention, regional; Magic is bred inherently—and differently—in the different territories of the GUE universe.

As we learned in Zork Nemesis, there is always a unified Harmony of the Spheres in operation in the Magical Atmosphere of the GUE—a greater harmony of balance composed from all of the metaphysical elements of the Zork Universe. Earth, Air, Fire, Water, and a fifth, more aetherial component, spoken of by mortals as Magic (or in ZN's alchemy, the "quintessence"). Now, we learn what happens when that Magic is completely removed from that harmonious equation.

When the Harmony of the Spheres—the natural balance between the physical and essential universe—is overtly disturbed for any noticeable length of time, the Magical Atmosphere of the GUE attempts to right itself. When the machinations of man or sorcerer preclude that self-regulation from taking place—as in the case of the Zork Inquisition—the Universe begins, quite literally, to unravel. The elements and essences begin to come apart at the seams.

As a result, the Harmony of Things Magical and Otherwise depends primarily upon a strict transactional barter system—a system of cosmic, global balance. The Metaphysics of Magic in the GUE is driven by an economy of finite resources: if a Wizard weaves a spell of alteration, creating wings on an animal that previously had none (say, for example, in the case of a lion that then becomes a griffin), then somewhere else in the universe a winged creature must lose its wings at the same time. And so it is with storms and becalmed waters; with bursting gardens and barren plots; with banished Magic and the Magic of revolution and return. Magic, and Magical States, are neither created nor destroyed; they are simply altered, summonsed, or pushed from sight.

Similarly, truly Magic persons cannot be destroyed in a traditional sense; or rather, their Magic cannot be. Long after the use-creature of the particular brand of Magic has been killed, their Magic will still exist, like a reverberation along a wire. Magic that was always will be. The issue becomes one of containment.

Schools Of Magic

There are four classes of GUE Magic, and four categories of GUE Spells, that pertain to this game. The three active classes of Magic that can be summonsed are: High Magic, Middle Magic, and Deep Magic. The fourth, a non-invocative category of utility Magic (administered by the Dungeon Master) is known as Use Magic.

High Magic

High Magic—sometimes referred to as Old Magic—is wild. Controlled by no wizard or mage, High Magic is best understood by Dragons, and by association, Griffs (though the knowledge of Griffs concerning High Magic is confined to scattered bits of Old Speech that are half hearsay and lore). High Magic is neither fundamentally good nor evil. Older than the Implementors themselves, High Magic is the wild stuff that the Empire was formed of—the uncontrollable, dangerous energy of Creation and Destruction, the Conjuration of the unknown from the known. High Magic also invokes Plant Growth & Communication Spells. Its powers are seemingly unlimited.

DISCLAIMER:

The Enchanters Guild, when in operation, sponsors all existing classes of Magic, and if given the chance, would in all likelihood seek to sponsor many more that do not in fact exist in any way, shape or form. (Disclaimer taken from Hyperbolic Incantation Concentrator.)

Old Speech, the runic language of dragons and some druids, details the power of High Magic—and lists the Names (true names, not call names) of every creature, animal, plant, or other property in the Empire. All Spells are first composed in Old Speech, and some can only be deciphered through Old Speech today.

High Magic is not traditionally associated with the Underground, as it takes its power from the unformed vastness of the Overland Sky. High Magic is dangerous, most of all to those who attempt to use it without fully understanding what they are doing, which is everyone who has ever attempted to use High Magic. Some Mithican creationist legends even go so far as to contend that the founding of the GUE itself is the result of one colossal malpractice of High Magic use.

Middle Magic

Middle Magic is the Mental Magic of Divination practiced by some Wizards and Enchanters, but also by the lower-ranking Telepaths—notably, Lucy Flathead, the tele-pathic halfling Flathead who accompanies you on your quest to return Magic to the Empire.

This Magic includes Magical Foresight, or Vision Quest, without even the aid of a Seer Stone; the Divination of Missings, Hiddens, and Invisibles; and the Memory of Unwitnessed Events.

Although Divination includes the Listening (to sounds unheard by human/creature ear—clairaudio) and the Seeing (of human/creature minds—clairvoyance) generally, it doesn't include the minds of animals and less-intelligent creatures, which just tend to come across as a great deal of static and chirping. Even reading the mind of a Brogmoid becomes difficult after a while; the laborious mental recitation "Step together and step together and step" can drown out any other productive thought he might (or might not) be having. Higher Mental Magic is naturally associated with a whole category of spells involving Mind Control and the manipulation of other persons and creatures.

Only those Diviners most trained in Mental Magic are capable of Seeing their own futures. Ultimately, Divination and Middle Magic is the Magic of Mortal Life, associated with the Middle World of the Overland, the above world of the GUE.

Deep Magic

Deep Magic is the Creature Magic of the Underground, of Transmutation and Enchantment, or Magical Change. Deep Magic includes Spells of Shape-Shifting, the Handling of Underground Animalia (conversing with animal/creatures, translating animal/creature behavior, taming animal/creatures), and the Compass of the Underground (the instinctive ability to divine direction in underground mazes and tunnels).

Deep Magic is also the Magic of the Underground Warrior, and much of it is understood instinctively by fighting races, including the Brogmoid. A creature like a Brogmoid would never be able to explain why it is he was able to know or do something, but he will know to do it, all the same.

Character Associations
The Dungeon Master

The DM, like all trained generalists in Magic, knows all the knowable Magic (which doesn't include all of the High Magic) and can weave any spell from any of the three classes of Magic. However, the current DM, Dalboz, seems most comfortable in his day-to-day life with a kind of lesser Old Magic; Dalboz is a Natural Mage who just seems to sprout magic wherever he goes. Still, he practices some of the seeing that a Diviner does, and knows much of the Deep Magic that would come naturally to an underground creature like a Brogmoid.

Most Wizards in Zork are like lawyers; they're specialists of Magic who have become so not because of any natural inclination, but because they studied at it. Dalboz, apart from the pack, is—like some of the Great Wizards before him—a Natural Mage, and thus we can deduce that he was born of the High Magic. But he is also quite fond of the arcane philosophizing recited by all Wizards, who have spent too long pursuing advanced degrees. Increasingly, and without exception, the longer a person has spent as a Wizard–even a Dungeon Master in waiting–the less a person will be able to perform certain common functions without Magic, like tie a good knot in a rope. Or, for that matter, tie shoelaces.

When enchanted and bodiless, there isn't a great deal of Magic the DM can practice, except perhaps to recollect certain Spells when his memory has been prompted by returning to enough of the terrain of the Empire.

Certainly, much of what comprises his Magic cannot be taken away from him with the absence of his body. For example, the DM always knows when Danger is near.

And the DM carries with him a formidable body of Magical knowledge–Astral (Astrology) and Elemental, Old Magic and New.

Also, the DM cannot be killed or destroyed because of the Long Life Spell he cast over himself just before the Closing of Magic.

The Griff

The powers of the Griff, and his sphere of knowledge, correspond with High Magic (see the preceding section on High Magic).

The Griff knows bits and snatches of Old Speech, which enables him to translate sections of spells and encrypted Magic riddles/objects. (Meaning the end game riddle engraved upon or accompanying the three Magic objects.) He loves Magic Objects and indeed, anything gold or jeweled, as a Crow would. Indeed, the insides of Griff nests (in the hollows of trees) are often veritable treasure troves, always handy for a few good Magical Objects.

The Griff can read the weather and predict it with some accuracy, he knows bits of a few good Growth Spells, and he has a good overall sense of the Big Picture of the Adventure, due to his aerial perspective on life (and the fact that he is about 350 years old.) He has an instinctive compass of OverLand (above the Underground) navigation, and is excellent at riddles, true to his breed. He is something of a Wit, as a result. He is interested in Magic, but fearful of its results–and far too neurotic to ever sleep.

Lucy Flathead

Lucy's powers, and her sphere of knowledge, are basically governed by the recognized laws of telepathy. However, her status as a halfling Flathead, and the enchanted blood of some sort of Wizard intertwined with her family lineage, makes her powers somewhat more vague. Her powers are the powers of Middle Magic, which is to say, Mental Magic (see the preceding section on Middle Magic). She can glimpse visions of the future, glimpse visions of the past, hear unheard sounds, see the invisible (doors, creatures, objects), and read minds (though not of animals. She can, however, sometimes subdue animals who are willing or educated enough to listen to reason).

THE BROGMOID

The Brogmoid's powers, and sphere of knowledge, correspond to the powers of Deep Magic, the Magic of the Underground (see the earlier section, Deep Magic). The Magic of the Underground involves transmutation and change. The Brog understands these spells and can recognize a shape-changer anywhere. He's about 200 years old, so you would think he would have gotten the hang of this whole Magic thing by now, but the Brogmoid is worse at Magic than anyone in your party. He's even worse with Magical Objects, and he can give you some really bad Magic Advice, so beware.

Once a part of Syovar III's honor guard, the Brog is the Warrior of the party. He's also gifted with a keen sense of right and wrong, an overwhelming compassion, and a sense of honor that is only slaked by revenge. He has an instinctive inner compass when in the Underground, so he can help the party from getting too lost in that region.

He loves all creatures, especially little animals, and he can tame any animal. He can read any animal environment and immediately know who has been there, and who they fear will come there—because he can speak the creature languages. Though he lives in a sod cave, rather than a glittering nest, the Brog loves jewels and metals as much as the Griff, and they tend to bicker over these. But the Brog always backs down if the Griff offers him a nice rock; Brogs love to pitch rocks more than anything else. You might not want to ask him a complicated physics problem about the nature of rock throwing, however. Or even how many fingers he has on his right hand. ("Which right hand?")

CHEAT SHEET

CHARACTER:	MAGIC TYPE:	CONTROLS:	ENVIRONMENT:
Griff	High	Creation & Destruction	Sky
Lucy Flathead	Middle	Divination & Enlightenment	Overland
Brogmoid	Deep	Transmutation & Enchantment	Underground

MAGIC OBJECTS

There are a host of magical treasures in the GUE, though at the time of ZGI most have been lost or banished and must be recovered and returned to the Empire in the name of restoring

Magic. The Coconut of Quendor, the Skull of Yoruk, and the Cube of Foundation are the three most important to ZGI.

The Coconut contains all of the Magic—that is, the Power of Magic—in the Empire. It is very much an artifact of Old Magic, and has been stolen back by the Dragons (the rightful stewards of the Coconut) until such a time as it can be restored to the GUE.

The Skull of Yoruk holds the key to all of the worldly Knowledge of Magic in the Empire. It is an artifact of Middle Magic, as it pertains to Mental Magic.

The Cube of Foundation, one of 17 such cubes, concerns the physical existence of the Empire. This Cube possesses Deep Magic.

Each magic object carries with it a part of a lost Rune of Abjuration, a sort of master magic spell woven in Old Speech between the three Magical Objects or Artifacts. When the three powerful Magic Objects are recovered at last, the Rune will summons Y'Gael back down from the Ethereal Planes of Atrii. When the three Magic Treasures are combined according to prophesy and the wisdom of Y'Gael, their essences will be freed, and Magic will return to the Empire.

More on the Subject of Magic

There is, of course, much more Magic than this in the Empire, but none more that you must know about for the purposes of Zork Grand Inquisitor; and were I to tell you any more, I would be tried as an Invoker myself, and Totemized without further ceremony. Of note, there is an entire genre of Warrior/Combat Magic; a dark practice of Necromantic Magic; the standard arrays of Healing Magic; the Elemental Magic (made familiar by the most popularized instance of Alchemy in the Forbidden Lands); and many more Guilds even than that. In fact, upon revisiting the issue, I am prompted to proclaim that there is entirely too much Magic in this land without Magic, and I believe that on concluding this document I will join the Inquisition myself.

* * *

Long Live Mir Yannick, the Grand High Inquisitor, and Leader of Peoples Away from Things Supernatural and thus Difficult to Understand and Write Upon!

Chapter VI:
The History of Zork

How to Distract a Grue: A Cumulative History of Zork

—by Antonius Hwarf

Throughout our long and tumultuous history, the more adventurous people of Zork—those daring enough to go wandering into the dark and uncharted regions of our realm, have been burdened by a constant danger. That being the irrepressible threat posed by a ravenously predatory creature called the grue. Dwelling exclusively in the darkest of darkness, no one has ever actually seen a grue. But judging by the extreme dearth of brave or adventurous souls in our land, it is obvious that their menace has taken its toll on the populace.

Since they were first discovered, many have sought ways to keep grues at bay. The Frobozz Magic Company created a spray-on substance called Froboz Magic Grue Repellent. This managed to do the job well enough, albeit for a matter of about thirty seconds. But Adventurers needed something that would last them through an entire day.

It was later declared by the Surgeon General of Greater Borphee, that the best way to avoid being eaten by a grue was to simply abstain from wandering into the darkest of dark places. But if one felt the undying urge to do so, they should make every attempt to bring some light-bearing object with them for protection, such as a lantern. Many Adventurers, however, still wouldn't listen.

In the hopes of finding a new way to keep from being eaten by a grue that will satisfy those who refuse to carry lanterns, I am submitting this very work. It has come to my attention that in the many attempts to cheat death while in the clutches of a grue, no one has ever tried distracting it with a nice, long, potentially sleep-inducing story. In my search for an adequately dreary topic, I have chosen to write about the history of our world, from its earliest beginnings up to the present day.[1]

CHAPTER VI: THE HISTORY OF ZORK

So if you do choose to go adventuring, and you find yourself in the clutches of a grue, seconds from being eaten; try pulling out this text and reading it.[2] And please let me know how it turns out.

Note: In the above circumstance, it would probably be best to skip this introduction.

The Coconut and Brogmoid Debate

Brogmoid or Coconut? Coconut or Brogmoid? The debate has raged on now for ages. Is the world of Zork perched on the shoulders of a giant Brogmoid, as two major episodes in Zork's history contend, or are we in fact clinging to the surface of a massive coconut that floats on an elliptical course around an even more massive watermelon? Differing views on the issue have polarized once unified and respected guilds, its theological and scientific implications have rocked our religious institutions and threaten to lay waste to centuries of research. Many a ponderous philosopher has fueled the fire with augmentative views. Even attempts at connecting the two beliefs have only worsened the situation. It is a fundamental question and, unfortunately, a necessary starting point for a cumulative history. What is the nature of the canvas upon which we have been rendered?

This is a dangerous topic to discuss in any literary work, as proponents for both sides of the debate are currently attempting to erase all texts that endorse the other side's theory. The slightest biased towards one side could lead to the permanent suppression of this entire volume. It is for this reason that I will make only passing references to this extremely relevant, yet equally volatile issue.

Geography

The world of Zork is divided into three major land masses—the Westlands, the Eastlands, and the island of Antharia—each separated by the body of water known as the Great Sea. The Westlands and the Eastlands are on opposite sides of the sea, with Antharia lying roughly halfway between these two continents.

The geography of Zork is well-defined, with the exception of two great mysteries that have been used, alternately, to perpetuate both the Coconut and Brogmoid theories.

What lies to the west of the Westlands? And what lies to the east of the Eastlands? Both continents are bordered on their outermost regions by treacherous mountain ranges. Expeditions have been launched, attempting to cross both sides, but none of these parties have ever been heard from again.

The coconut zealots claim that the two mountain ranges are the same, and that crossing one side will lead directly to the other continent. The brogmoid fundamentalists insist that these are the edges of the world, and that beyond them lie a great void of nothingness.

Ancient Civilizations

The realm of Zork is littered, as any self-respecting civilization should be, with an assortment of mysterious and ancient predecessors whose origins date back to long before the reign of Entharion. Their various remnants can be seen in the landscape, language, and lore of Quendor.

Borphee and Pheebor

The Borphee Province in the Westlands contains the oldest surviving city in the entire realm of Quendor. Its breathtaking marble temples and magnificent coliseums constructed out of dornbeast tusks have been declared the foundation of modern society. In fact, all known clusters of civilization can be traced back to this culture. But its prominence did not come undisputed.

The city was built at the end of the great Borphee River, which runs across the Westland region and empties into the Great Sea. In the early days of Borphee, the river indirectly provided all of the city's resources, and is still treated with an almost godlike reverence by the Borpheans. They were an autonomous people, free from interest or concern about the outside world.

On the other end of the Westlands, at the point where the various tributaries flow together to form the beginning of the river, there existed a twin city called Pheebor[3] which, incidentally, regarded the river with much the same reverence. At the time, both cities had called the magnificent waterway the One River. But in a tragic fit of self-importance, occurring around 400 B.E. (Before Entharion), the two groups simultaneously decided to rename the river after their own city. Both cities were, of course, deeply offended by the other's selfishness and a bloody battle ensued.

The two forces met in the southern plains of Egreth, roughly halfway between the two cities. The Pheeborians, led by the irreversible yet tremendously incapable, Prince Foo, stood on the northern side of the deep ravine that contained the One River. The Borpheans, led by the uncommonly clever General Horteus Shplee, took their place on the southern side. The general was a shrewd war strategist, well aware of his subtle tactical advantage. The two armies charged, swords drawn. But the excitement of the moment was quickly dowsed when both sides reached the river and were forced to dive in and paddle awkwardly towards each other. Instead of meeting in the glorious clash of steel that all had hoped for, it appeared more like a graceless collision of drowning fools. The armies splashed frantically at each other, hardly noticing the effect of the river's strong current. An effect that General Shplee had been counting on.

The cluster of bobbing heads drifted rapidly downstream towards Borphee, where a battalion of Shplee's men waited with a stockade of granite rocks. As the soldiers floated by, the battalion tossed the rocks at the Pheeborian army, apparently enjoying themselves enormously in the process and not worrying too much about the many Borphean soldiers that were mixed in with the bunch. This tactic proved quite successful, and is credited with bringing a very quick end to what would have likely ended up being a long and pointless war. Prince Foo was promptly beheaded by one of the more zealous (and buoyant) Borphean knights. And the city of Pheebor fell a few days later.

So thorough was the Borphean army's gleeful ransacking of Pheebor, that the entire body of knowledge accumulated by this once great people was completely wiped out.

All that was left after one night of devastation was a few scattered ruins and a number of unanswered questions. Hence, the people of Pheebor are still regarded with a sense of curious wonder today.

The Mithican Tribes

It has been quietly acknowledged by some of the more progressive enchanters that the linguistical root of Magic, commonly known as the Old Tongue, is the same language once used by the Mithican Tribes. This was quite a scandalous assertion when it first surfaced, during the early Ninth Century. Many conservative guild members felt that it was blasphemous to attribute such credit to a group of people who had been perceived as savage and culturally inconsequential up until that point. The Mithicans lived in primitive huts, wore vulgar loincloths, and derived entertainment from sitting around a bonfire, yelling and hollering at the sky. They couldn't possibly have developed such an enlightened understanding of the universe. But the words of the renowned historian, Ozmar, in 821 GUE, held great sway. "The ancients of our kind were nearer to knowing the truth about Science than those who we call Scientists today."

Before the guild of anthropologists made their discovery, the Mithican dialect was thought to have been survived only by the title of the game, Snarfem, a common source of entertainment along the streets of many major cities. All that was known about this mysterious group was that they lived apart from the relatively metropolitan areas of Borphee and Pheebor, along the outskirts of the Miznia forest, and had been there since long before either city's people had ascended beyond incessant grunting and formed the first semblance of a society.

It is now known, however, that the seemingly awkward, runic words used by sorcerers and enchanters to invoke magic spells during the era of thaumaturgy are the same words that were incorporated into every day Mithican life. Magic flowed through the Mithican people with amazing intensity. Virtually everything that was said by a tribesperson had the accidental side effect of invoking some potentially dangerous spell. This is thought to have caused many problems for the Mithicans, and is probably the reason for their mysterious disappearance around the time of 800 B.E. It is also an excellent demonstration of the perils inherent in Magic usage that, were it not for the whole Magic debacle of 966 GUE and the guiding hand of the Grand Inquisitor, would have most likely destroyed our entire society.

Centuries after their disappearance, the two main villages of the Mithican tribes were found and utilized by settlers who left Borphee in search of more stuff. They named the two villages Gurth and Mithicus. Since then, the two provinces have become a haven for artisans, and the Fields of Frotzen, located within Gurth, are renowned for their incredible agricultural capacity. Seeds that are planted within the fields often ripen within days. This attribute has made it the second most abundant agricultural resource in the Westlands.

THE EASTLANDS

As all this was happening, life in the Eastlands remained quite sedate. The scattered enclaves of humanoids who were indigenous to the continent are referred to in all historical accounts as simply, "the natives," and were said to be quite easy going people. Hence, they were doomed from the moment Duncanhrax's ships hit the shore, but we'll get to that later.

Other less sentient beings who occupied the land, such as trolls and gnomes, were kept alive during the Duncanthrax Conquests both for manual labor and for their inherent novelty.

THE MASHED POTATO WARS

In the ensuing vanity following Pheebor's defeat in 400 B.E., the Borpheans became rather excited about the notion of conquering new lands. After countless humbly uninquisitive generations, the population had flourished and the people were suddenly curious about what else lay beyond their borders. The first wave of settlers discovered the remnants of Gurth and Mithica. And a short time later, a second expedition made an incredible discovery that would permanently change both the economic and culinary structure of the Westlands.

The head of the expedition, a courageous, stoic and highly admired noble named Sir Thaddeus Galepath, described their finding in his journal. "Neither I, nor any of the men had believed a word of the scout's barely coherent mutterings. But his dumbfounded elation was at least matched by my own reaction upon reaching the hilltop and standing before the field of mushy white substance. In blatant, but understandable, disregard for my orders, the men dropped their belongings and charged down the hill. I quickly gathered my senses and followed behind them. After testing the consistency of the substance with our hands, we threw caution to the wind and dove headlong into what we soon discovered to be the most delicious mashed potatoes that any of us had ever tasted."

When news (and abundant samples) of this phenomena were sent to Borphee, the ruler of the burgeoning empire, a man named Mareilon, ordered that a village be established immediately to harvest the mashed potatoes and send regular shipments back to Borphee in lieu of any monetary taxation, and that the village be named in his honor. Upon receiving these orders, Sir Galepath realized that there must have been some kind of miscommunication, as he had already built an encampment which his men had fondly named, Galepath. It was also his understanding that Galepath would be a separate city, free from any kind of taxation and interacting with the other cities by way of equally balanced trade of goods. The dialogue between the two men quickly turned ugly and became steadily worse as it approached what seemed to be an inevitable war.

Fearing a repeat of the Pheebor massacre, Galepath's advisors convinced him to invite Mareilon to a summit, where they would put their egos aside and work out their problems. Needless to say, this did not work. But surprisingly, it was not a complete disaster. Mareilon returned to Borphee, absorbed by this development, and quickly assembled another expedition that would colonize the region just south of Galepath. This new city would fall directly under Mareilon's reign, as it was to be overseen by him, personally.

The competition between the cities of Galepath and Mareilon escalated over the years, eventually outlasting both men's lives. Though the mashed potato fields were virtually boundless, spiteful citizens would often harvest from the other city's fields. Despite the valiant attempt to resolve the issue early on, war eventually did break out. But by this time, the new ruler of Borphee had wisely detached himself from the feud, thereby drastically lowering the stakes.

The cities of Galepath and Mareilon fought for centuries. And as they did so, both sides slowly lost touch with why they were fighting to begin with. They were driven by a self-perpetuating and meaningless anger that only seemed to grow stronger after losing its foundation. The cities grew in equal proportion to their citizens' disdain of the enemy, until both lands surpassed even Borphee in size.

"Why Fight?"

When the year 0 GUE finally came around, the people of Zork felt fairly certain that something big was about to happen. This assumption turned out to be true, as it has since become known as the year that a young man named Entharion emerged from Egreth Forest and built himself a tiny hut on the beach between Galepath and Mareilon.

Stunned by the presence of their new neighbor. Soldiers from both cities approached the hut. They took turns interrogating Entharion. The Galepathians would poke his left shoulder with their spears and ask him where he came from, then before he could answer, the Mareilonians would poke his right shoulder and demand to know who had sent him. This went on for some time, until Entharion, instead of answering any of the questions, inquired about the apparent hostility between the two groups of soldiers. One of the dozen or so men crammed inside the tiny hut explained that they had been in a war for hundreds of years, noting, however, that it was none of his business and that he better get to answering their questions right away. Disobeying this order, Entharion again asked a question. "Why Fight?"

From that day forth, the modest, unassuming man who emerged from the woods was known as Entharion the Wise. With a perfectly naive question, Entharion brought peace to a wartorn land and began a dynasty that reigned over the entire realm and would continue to hold the thrown for over 600 years.

It was a glorious time. The new kingdom was named Quendor, for no particular reason, and Entharion's castle was erected between the cities he'd united, on the former site of his hut. The region surrounding the castle was named Largoneth, also for no particular reason.

The Entharion Dynasty

The rule of Entharion fostered a period of peaceful resolve from the seemingly endless strife that had preceded it. With the concerns that accompany constant warfare thrown aside, people in all the cities of Quendor were able to concentrate on more academic subjects. There was a sudden curiosity about the nature of the world. The literary works that were produced during this period mark the very beginnings of what later became known as Thaumaturgy; the experimental study of applied magic.

Entharion married Queen Lynpo, a direct descendant of Galepath, and fathered one son before his magnificent reign ended in 41 GUE.[4] He was succeeded by his son, Mysterion the Brave, of whom little is known other than his general bravery. Equally little is known about his successor, Zylon the Aged, who held the throne for a staggering 344 years before finally conceding to the seemingly unspoken guidelines regarding human longevity.

This trend of fairly uneventful reigns continued throughout the Entharion Dynasty. It was a period of remarkable social dullness. A few scattered events, such as the Zuchinni Wars, galvanized the public interest, but these spasms of misdirected strife were predominantly unsuccessful and invariably short-lived.

THE EMPIRICAL AGE

As political matters remained stagnant, however, academic institutions were advancing in leaps and bounds. Many scholars felt that they had finally begun to achieve some understanding of an underlying order in the seemingly chaotic world. This period of enlightenment is now referred to as the Empirical Age, and it was during this time that many important scientific discoveries and technological innovations were made.

Astronomers began meticulously analyzing the motion of celestial bodies, physicists made stunning assertions about the apparent tendency of all things to "gravitate" towards the ground and cartographers insisted that their geographical surveys simply didn't add up under the assumption that Zork lay on a flat surface. All these things combined to give rise to the Giant Coconut theory, which enjoyed uncontested dominance in all academic circles up until the late Fourth Century. These stirring events were quickly answering the great mysteries of the ages that had baffled mankind.

This would seem to have been a fascinating era to be alive, but alas, it was still pretty dull. Perhaps it was this very dullness which prompted two of the most important events in Zork's history.

YORUK CROSSES THE SEA

Born in 353, towards the end of Zylon's mercilessly boring rule, Yoruk was a perfectly obscure mashed potato merchant from Galepath. But even at a young age, it was clear that he was not cut out for the work. In the hackneyed lifestyle of a potato merchant, there was little use for Yoruk's keen ability to reason and deduce. He grew tired of his dreary, secure life, and spent most of his day in a catatonic stupor. "This can't be it!" were the last words anyone heard him say before he stormed out of Galepth's mashed potato district, flailing his arms wildly.

Yoruk fled to the shore and stared out at the Great Sea. It was an endless expanse whose boundaries had never been explored. What lay beyond the Great Sea? It seemed, to him, the only great mystery in the world worth solving.

Yoruk began building himself a raft. He reasoned that if he tied a few pieces of wood together and held a large bedsheet up with a stick, the wind would carry him out to sea. He wasn't quite sure how he would bring himself back, but he reasoned that if he couldn't find anything of interest beyond the horizon, he wouldn't have much interest in returning home anyway. He went home for just long enough to grab a saw, a bedsheet and a sack filled with as much mashed potatoes as he could carry, then headed into he forest to chop down a tree.

In 380 GUE, Yoruk pushed his raft out to sea. Two days later, his raft snapped and sank, spelling certain death for its aquatically-uninclined passenger. But as luck would have it, Yoruk did not die. As he sank into the infinite depths, his hand latched onto a pliant, fleshy growth on the side of some larger body that was cruising by beneath the surface. Yoruk held on for dear life as the creature darted through the water, frequently rising to the surface and allowing Yoruk a chance to breathe. This went on for days, and through it all, Yoruk maintained his grip on the creature, but was never able to open his eyes and see what it was that he was riding.

Yoruk finally lost both his grip and his consciousness before reaching any sign of land. But when he awoke after an indeterminate slumber, he was lying safely on an unknown shore. He had crossed the Great Sea and arrived in the Eastlands. And in his hand he found a shard of an ivory-like substance that seemed to have broken off of some giant tooth. It was exquisitely smooth, as if it had been carved by hand into the shape of a dagger. He kept it, reasoning that it might be a useful thing to have.

Beyond the Endless Expanse

Standing on the shore of the Eastlands, looking out at the water, Yoruk was quite pleased with himself. He had crossed the infinite sea. He had stretched the edge of his world by an incredible distance and answered an ancient question. But still, he was not content. There were many more questions that needed answering. The scientists of Galepath had made bold attempts at defining the world of Zork, but none were to Yoruk's satisfaction. For example, if the world was indeed clinging to the surface of a giant coconut, why did the water in the Great Sea not fall off to the side?[5] And if diseases were truly caused by so-called 'germs' on his body, why did they not drown when he bathed?[6] Certainly, there was much more knowledge to be acquired.

Yoruk found a small, damp cave beside a mountain in the region just south of what is now called Port Foozle, and made it his home. During the day, he wandered the realm, pondering these questions as he hunted for food with the help of his trusty dagger. At night, he slept safely in his cave.

One evening, just before going to bed, Yoruk heard a visitor enter his cave. He quickly doused his fire and crept into a corner. He watched the visitor step closer, and as it drew near, he was able to make out a faint silhouette. The visitor was of average height and build, but it seemed to have two sharp horns protruding from its forehead, and Yoruk felt quite certain that he spotted a set of enormous, featherless wings attached to the visitor's back. Yoruk soon realized that he was sharing a cave with a daemon. Fortunately, it seemed to have no knowledge of his presence. The daemon passed right by him and continued deeper into the cave, faintly lighting the way with the reddish glow it emitted from its eyes.

Yoruk's Descent Into the Underworld

As he crouched in his corner, Yoruk reasoned that the cave must be an entranceway into Hades, and if he quietly followed the daemon, he might be able to gain access into the nether world. He also reasoned that the Devil, being the Devil, would probably keep less exclusive company than the all-powerful Implementors, and would therefore be a pretty good resource for the knowledge that he sought.

He followed the daemon as it crept through the dark caves, gradually descending deeper and deeper beneath the surface world. Yoruk always kept a fair distance behind it and was careful not to make any jarring noises that might alert the daemon to his presence. As they descended, Yoruk was led through breathtaking caverns, gorges, and canyons. They passed areas that were teeming with life of a strange and magical sort. But Yoruk could only pay quick notice to these things, because the daemon kept a swift pace.

As they descended further, Yoruk noticed that the walls were gaining a reddish hue, and the heat was reaching a somewhat unbearable level. But he pressed on, driven by curiosity. After several days of walking, the daemon finally reached the gates of Hades, which stood directly behind a large ring of fire, and directly in front of an enormous, fire-snarling, three-headed serpent-beast known as the Great Daemon of the Threshold. The lesser daemon reached into the sack that it carried and pulled out a large shield. It lifted the shield and leapt through the ring of fire, then through the gates and past the enormous, fire-snarling, three-headed serpent-beast known as the Great Daemon of the Threshold.

Yoruk was astonished by this feat. Knowing full-well that it was beyond the meager skills that he had acquired as a mashed potato merchant to leap through a ring of fire, he simply stood in awe. As he did so, an assortment of ghouls, monsters and other lesser daemons circled around him. In his dazed stupor, Yoruk didn't notice that they were closing in on him. He didn't notice their presence at all, for that matter. It wasn't until the last moment, just before they began gnawing on his head, that he realized he'd been spotted.

He swung his arms in all directions, inadvertently poking a giant hellhound in the eye and, in the process, releasing its vice-like grip on his cranium. He then blindly reached out and grabbed one of the lesser daemons' shields from its hands. After plowing through an assortment of drooling zombies with his shield raised, he leapt through the ring of fire, then through the gates of Hades and almost made it past the enormous, fire-snarling, three-headed serpent-beast known as the Great Daemon of the Threshold.

When Yoruk came to his senses, he looked up and realized that the Great Daemon of the Threshold, anticipating his arrival, had stepped into his path and blocked him with its tremendous stomach. He lay on the steaming hot ground, at the Great Daemon of the Threshold's feet.[7] The Great Daemon laughed as Yoruk scrambled to his feet,[8] and it laughed when Yoruk pulled out the shard of a giant tooth that he had found in his hand on the shore of the Eastlands, but it did not laugh when Yoruk swiftly stuck the shard into its tremendous stomach.

The enormous, fire-snarling, three-headed serpent-beast known as the Great Daemon of the Threshold flailed wildly for several minutes, partially out of pain and suffering, partially out of shock, and partially because it just enjoyed the melodrama of it all. Regardless, it eventually laid down, thoroughly dead.

He Who Knows the Ways of Deep Magic

Yoruk had no idea that the Devil had been watching his escapades all along, nor did he know that the Devil was actually quite amused. When the Great Daemon finally died, the Devil emerged from the shadows and brought Yoruk down to his lair. The two got along splendidly and soon became very good friends. In time, the Devil imparted his knowledge of all things to Yoruk. This included an extended session on the topic of Deep Magic, one of the three kinds of Magic that flows through the cosmos, and the one that is commonly linked to the dark ways of those who dwell in the underworld.

Years later, Yoruk left Hades and returned to the surface world. Armed with an implicit understanding of the universe and its workings, Yoruk made a far better sailor than before, so he was able to construct a new and much more seaworthy vessel in a very short time. He returned to the shores of Galepath, but instead of marching into the city and gaining instant fame for his knowledge, he built himself a modest cottage in the forests of Egreth where he lived out the rest of his natural life. From 406 to his death in 425, he wrote what is known as the *Books of Saint Yoruk*. The Books of Saint Yoruk are filled with fascinating revelations, but they are most often cited as the source of the Great Brogmoid theory, one of the great many things that he learned under the Devil's tutelage.

THE SKULL OF YORUK

Legend has it that Yoruk's adventures continued on well after his death, with his transcendence to the Ethereal Plains of Atrii, and his strange encounter with the Implementors. They had taken an interest in him after watching his exploits, and brought him to their far away realm as a guest. Surprisingly, Yoruk was none too impressed with them and asked to be returned to Hades. The Implementors were terribly offended and refused to grant him his wish, so Yoruk headed off on his own to find his way back.

Though his spirit is said to still wander, his knowledge was imprinted within his corpse. Thus, the Skull of Saint Yoruk has become one of the most coveted and sought after relics in all the Empire. Its bearer wields the knowledge and power of Deep Magic. The Skull has been in the possession of many celebrated figures throughout history, eventually ending up in the clutches of the second Dungeon Master in 948 GUE, but it disappeared a short time later and was never heard from again.

PILGRIMAGE TO HADES

By the mid-fifth century, the Books of Yoruk had grown quite a following. Those who sought adventure, as Yoruk once had, found it within his words. Those who sought answers, as Yoruk once had, found those as well. And those who sought proof of Yoruk's claims, as much of Quendor had begun to, built ships to retrace his path. Assuming that they would not be graced with Yoruk's incredibly good fortune, the crafts would have to be far more seaworthy than his humble raft. A great number of innovators applied the breadth of technology in the realm and, in 454, the largest fleet of ships ever assembled set off on a pilgrimage to the Eastlands.

Most of the ships sank within the first week, and when a sailor on one of the few over-crowded vessels that remained spotted a land mass on the horizon, no one dared to ask if it was the one they were looking for. The currents had brought them to the island of Antharia. While only 959 square bloits[9] in size, the beautiful landscape and near-perfect weather quickly became known as home to the unwitting colonists. Relying heavily on the sea's bounty, they built a quaintly misanthropic civilization, exhibiting no interest in maintaining contact with the homeland. They left in search of enlightenment and accidentally found paradise instead.

Over the centuries, sporadic attempts by the Quendorians to set foot on Antharian soil prompted them to build a powerful navy that guarded the coast. This thoroughly irritated Thaddium Fzort, the ninth king of the Entharion Dynasty, but like all the other kings of his time, he didn't want to get his subjects riled and have to start an unnecessary war.

Thaumaturgy: The Study of Incredibly Weird Stuff

After Yoruk's adventures, the second major development that came out of the irksome Entharion bloodline was the heightened interest in some peculiar and often handy effects that could be gained by uttering strange words, spoken in what was then called the Old Tongue. The subject was formally dubbed Thaumaturgy, and its canonical work was written in 473 GUE by a professor at Galepath University, named Bizboz.

On the Presence of Incredibly Weird Stuff Going On remains the most heavily scrutinized and controversial scientific study ever published. In it, Bizboz claimed to have discovered "for-the-most-part natural rules" that explained the "Weird Stuff" which he and several other deviant researchers had been experimenting with. He claimed to have harnessed a natural energy, called Magic, and used it to create "spells." The book gave long dissertations on the useful applications of spells like nerzo, for balancing checkbooks; umboz, for tedious housecleaning duties; and yumzo, for destroying mongeese.

Though his technique was undeniably fruitful and his research infallible, Bizboz was ostracized by his colleagues and laughed out of Galepath University. His findings blatantly contradicted the teachings of almost every professor at the University. They refused to even waste their time "rationalizing his nonsense."

Within months, Bizboz was stripped of all he had and reduced to panhandling on the street. His "Weird Stuff" had become nothing more than a label for the potions and powders, sold by charlatans, that would supposedly cure the ills of suffering peasants. Tragically, Bizboz committed suicide in 475. He never lived to see his pioneering work embraced by the community that once scorned him. Centuries later, Ozmar would say this of his work: "Science has taught us much and given us new words for old mysteries.

But beneath these words are mysteries, and beneath them more mysteries. The pursuit of Magic has given those mysteries meaning and provided for our people great benefits unrealized as yet by Science…We owe a great debt to Bizboz."

MEANWHILE, 184 YEARS LATER

The Entharion Dynasty remained stabile through several more kings. A total of 13, in all, had held the throne before Zilbo III succeeded Mumbo II in 628. Zilbo was a pleasant, agreeable, well-mannered king. In other words, he was boring beyond the realm of any Quendorian citizen's tolerance, and on the last day of 659 GUE, they revolted. Led by a power-hungry young zealot named Duncanthrax, the proletariat stormed Castle Largoneth, furious over an alleged shortage of mosquito netting. But in truth, the people were just desperate for a more interesting ruler. Conveniently, Duncanthrax declared himself the new King of Quendor upon beheading Zilbo III.

In his coronation speech, he declared, "I, King Duncanthrax, vow that I will stop at nothing to fulfill my every whim. Every petty longing, every outrageous desire, will be tasked upon my loving kingdom to fulfill. I also vow that my children, and my children's children will be raised with the very same values."

The cheering masses were enthralled by his naturally abusive behavior. They finally had a ruler who would keep them on their toes. And that he did.

One of Duncanthrax's first acts as King was to move the castle from Largoneth to Egreth. The people were pleased by this decree, but they absolutely swooned when he insisted that the job be done without disassembling a single piece of the castle. On several occasions during the moving process, entire legions of workers were crushed beneath the awkwardly mobile palace. Within the first six months of his rule, Duncanthrax the Bellicose, as he became known, had caused more unnecessary deaths than the entire Entharion Dynasty combined.

Upon settling down in Egreth, one of Duncanthrax's first tasks was to start a family. This was something he took very seriously. He announced to his kingdom that he was to be the first king of the Flathead Dynasty. This took the people by surprise, as it was not known to be a part of his title, nor was it at all indicative of the clearly non-flat shape of

179

his head. He declared that from then on, the flatness of ones head was to be directly correlated with their royal stature, and that he sought the most flatheaded woman in the land to be his queen. The call went out across the Westlands and in a very short time, Duncanthrax had found and married a particularly flatheaded and very stunned young lady from Mareilon, named Salestra. They were married immediately, and within a year they had their first son. The boy was named Belwit the Flat, and much to Duncanthrax's pleasure, his head did indeed have a somewhat flat shape to it.

Expanding the Empire

A few years after ascending the throne. Duncanthrax became dissatisfied with the size of his empire. The nation of Quendor did span across every inch of the Westlands, but the exploits of Yoruk had yielded two great land masses that had not yet been conquered.

He first set his mind to defeating the Antharian Armada, which had grown quite large in the centuries since the island was first settled. He put his best engineers to the task of creating ships that could overwhelm the Antharians, and by 665 he felt confident that they could pull it off.

The ships were put to the test during the battle of Fort Griffspotter, later that year. Duncanthrax's fleet closed in on the Antharian shore, but the Fort's long barrel guns kept him at bay. The ships were clearly no match for the Antharian war machine and would have met a quick fate were it not for Duncanthrax's clever back-up plan. He had secretly sent a ship full of spies in Antharian uniforms to the island nation, several months prior to the invasion. They carefully infiltrated the ranks and took posts within Fort Griffspotter, then at the key moment, they took out the gunners, allowing Duncanthrax to move his ships into firing range. Unaware of this subterfuge, Duncanthrax's fleet let loose on the Fort upon sinking the opposing battleships. The spies were killed in the shelling along with the remaining Antharian soldiers, and the tactic remained secret long enough for the reputation of the Quendorian Navy's might to spread back to the homeland.

By borrowing from Fort Griffspotter's vast armory and creating manufacturing facilities that mimicked the Antharian's advanced weapons technology, Duncanthrax's ground forces were able to hold their ground against the Antharian army's retaliation. Thus began the bloodiest battle in the history of Zork. Eventually, Duncanthrax's troops managed to quash every remaining enclave of the Antharian forces, giving them undisputed control of the granola mines as well as the Great Sea.

"Onward, to the Eastlands!"

Still bothered by the alleged existence of the Eastlands, Duncanthrax directed his ships in its direction. They hit the shore in 666 and instantly began ransacking whatever shreds of pre-existing civilization they could find. What few armed resistance movements there were didn't last very long. The strongest militia that the "natives" were able to pull together assembled at Zorbel Pass to face Duncanthrax's forces.

The natives entrenched themselves at the exit of the narrow path and managed to keep the enemy at bay, taking advantage of the narrow battleground to limit the size of Duncanthrax's vanguard to only a few men at a time. Duncanthrax responded by ordering the majority of his troops to pull out of the gorge. The natives, thinking they had forced a retreat, began a pell-mell pursuit of the remaining forces that led them through the pass and out into the fields beyond. Duncanthrax's army surrounded them on open ground then swiftly cut through their meager ranks. The remaining portions of the Eastlands were conquered without much difficulty.

While scouring the landscape for signs of where Yoruk began his fabled descent into Hades, Duncanthrax's soldiers stumbled into an intricate network of caverns and tunnels that spanned across the entire continent. This discovery came at exactly the right time for Duncanthrax, as he had recently become depressed after conquering every territory on the surface of Zork and having nothing left to do. He was inspired by the endless passageways, realizing that by digging even more, he could expand the size of his empire by five—or even tenfold.

Work began on the new underground tunnels in 668 GUE, with the creation of the Frobozz Magic Cave Company. The company almost immediately spawned two subsidiaries; the Frobozz Magic Dirt Removal Company and the Frobozz Magic Underground Sewer Installation Company. Within the year, FrobozzCo International was formed as a parent company for the burgeoning subsidiaries. By 743, FrobozzCo International oversaw more than 17,000 subsidiaries.

In an eight year span, King Duncanthrax the Bellicose expanded the nation of Quendor across all of Zork. By all accounts, the empire had reached its zenith. At long last, he retired to his castle at Egreth in 670, victorious.

The Unnatural Acts

Upon returning to his homeland, Duncanthrax found that the "Weird Stuff" of Bizboz's writings had spread like a cancer during his absence. Many of his subjects had taken to the liberal use of scrolls, potions, and powders for everyday needs. These unskilled sorcerers were inadvertently wreaking havoc on the land. Something had to be done.

In 672, Duncanthrax passed the Unnatural Acts, which put heavy restraints on the unauthorized use of Magic and threatened severe penalties for anyone caught selling "Unnatural or Supernatural substances." This was to be his last significant act as king. In 688, after a long stretch of relatively non-bellicose activity, Duncanthrax passed away, leaving the throne for his first son, Belwit the Flat.

The Scientific Age

Belwit's 13 year reign contained three important events. The increasingly popular card game, Double Fanucci, had its first championship competition in Borphee. The zorkmid, Quendor's primary form of currency, was minted. And toward the end of Belwit's short reign came the dawning of the Scientific Age. Serious students from such sacred institutions as Galepath University and Mithicus Province University took up the study of Thaumaturgy in their spare time. Eventually, some of these students achieved high-ranking positions on the faculties of several moss-league colleges, and Bizboz's long-ridiculed work finally gained public acceptance.

Toward the end of the seventh century, the new perception of Magic caused a loosening of the Unnatural Acts. This allowed Magic to be practiced and experimented with by an ordained institution called the Enchanters' Guild. The first and most famous house of the Enchanters' Guild was established in the small town of Accardi-By-The-Sea by the renowned thaumaturge, Vilboz.

It was found that the act of casting a spell required three important steps. These were known as Presence, Incantation, and Unusual Effect. It was also found that the reason Thaumaturgists were having such trouble casting spells was because they had no reliable way of completing the first step. This problem was first dealt with in 723, with the invention of the Hyperbolic Incantation Generator, better known as the magic wand. It gained enormous respect for the fledgling science which had, up until that point, yielded no marketable products.

With Belwit's son, Frobwit the Flatter came an even less restrained appreciation for Magic, as well as an even flatter head.

Another Advancement in the Production of Magic Spells

Another advancement in the production of magic spells occurred during the reign of King Mumberthrax the Insignificant. Working in the newly crowned king's laboratory, a thaumaturge named Davmar discovered a means by which Incantation could be stored on a special Presence-imbued paper. These so-called "scrolls" were found, however, to be destroyed during the spells' Incantation. Nonetheless, scrolls soon replaced the temperamental Hyperbolic Incantation Generator as the primary means of Incantation.

This development brought cheaper, easier, and more reliable spellcasting to the people. However, the fact that scrolls could be used only once remained a great frustration that prevented many people from bothering with them.

The Twelve Flatheads

Mumberthrax the Insignificant fathers the Twelve Flatheads. Dimwit is first, followed by 11 eclectically distinguished siblings: a captain of industry, a military hero, a musical genius, a dauntless banker and financier, an inventor extraordinaire, an artist and scientist, a chronic widow, a poet, a seaman and explorer, a royal architect, and a legendary athlete.

Each played a role in the most romanticized era of Zork's history, the reign of Lord Dimwit Flathead.

THE INDUSTRIAL AGE

The brief period known as the Industrial Age began in 769 GUE, just before Dimwit took the throne, with a discovery made by an unrecognized practitioner of the thaumaturgical arts named Berzio. Working for years in his own self-made workshop and often going for days without food, drink, or sleep, Berzio created the means by which the Presence of any of the lesser spells could be transferred from a scroll to a specially imbued paper by use of a simple spell, which he named after his dog, Gnusto. This paper, in turn, held the Presence even after the Incantation had been finished, solving the major problem in spell production. This gave rise to "spell books," which were capable of holding dozens of spells. Thaumaturgy had yielded its second great money-making product, one that could stand as the foundation for an entire industry.

The Industrial Age also saw the sublimation of formerly disreputable potions and powders that contained magical Presence. Once sold only by peddlers on the street, these items became second only to the spell book in popularity. The first over-the-counter potion was given the name Berzio, in honor of the great Thaumaturge.

LORD DIMWIT FLATHEAD THE EXCESSIVE

In all the years of the empire, through all of its eccentrics, no one comes close to matching the inimitable mark made by Lord Dimwit Flathead the Excessive. No ego, no vanity, no exaggerated sense of proportion can compare with the likes of the man who cleared 1400 square bloits of vegetation in the Fublio Valley to make way for a nine-bloit-tall statue of himself.

Dimwit grew up a tad spoiled. He shared the fondness of his great great great great grandfather, Kind Duncanthrax, for the uncharted territories of the Eastlands and its myriad caves and tunnels. He spent much of his early adulthood vacationing across the sea with 40,000 of his closest friends, and when his father passed away in 770, leaving Dimwit as king, he immediately relocated the capital to the little-known colony of Aragain in the central Eastlands. The small hamlet was replaced with the 8600 square bloit monstrosity known as Castle Flatheadia, which housed over 90% of the empire's population. He also declared that the empire of Quendor was to be renamed "The Great

Underground Empire" in both its above and below ground regions. This was a great relief to the people, as it shed light on the mysterious acronym that had followed the year since the reign of Entharion.

A short time later, planning began for Dimwit's official coronation, an event of such monumental importance that the 18-month festivity took 13 years to prepare, thereby placing it well into the latter half of his reign. In fact, the beginning and end of the coronation planning process act as bookends to achievements for which Lord Dimwit is best known.

LUCREZIA IMPRISONED

Though there has never been an accurate count, it is known that the Flatheadia Dungeon (also known as the Asylum), completed in 771, contained no less than 10,000 occupants at its peak. This is of minor historical note in the context of Dimwit's other acts of excessiveness, but it is worth mentioning because of a drama that played itself out within the dungeon's walls.

After all of her eighteen marriages came to grisly ends, with each husband being gruesomely killed in increasingly bizarre accidents, Lucrezia Flathead, the tenth sibling of the Twelve Flatheads, was rumored to be in a miserable emotional state. Fearing her suicide, the über-widow was imprisoned in the dungeon by Dimwit himself, though it pained him dearly. In search of comforting for her misery, Lucrezia had an insatiable fondness for prison guards. Coincidentally, 1800 prison guards were mysteriously poisoned in the years following her imprisonment. But it wasn't a prison guard for whom she felt her deepest love; it was a fellow inmate, who had been imprisoned for his flagrant overuse of Magic without proper consent by the Enchanters' Guild.

The two met frequently during Lucrezia's 15 years in the Flatheadia Dungeon. Surprisingly, the enchanter did not die. It is even rumored that he lived to see Lucrezia give birth to their daughter and made a daring escape soon after, with their child in tow. Beyond this, nothing is known, but speculation abounds as to what happened to the lost Flathead.

The Endless Fire of Mareilon

In 773, the public's acceptance of magic was set back by a slight mispronunciation and its rather severe consequences. A well-meaning Mareilonian civil servant was apparently attempting to cast a spell called Zemdor (turn original into triplicate), but accidentally spoke the word Zimbor (turn one really big city into lots of tiny, little ashes) instead. After a blazing inferno that lasted 4 weeks, the city was destroyed.

Lord Dimwit's response was swift and characteristically extreme. In the weeks following the Fire, Dimwit issued 5,521 edicts which had the effect of severely limiting public access to magic. Henceforth, all magic was entrusted to the enchanters' guilds, which had, by then, opened chapters in most cities and towns.

"My Best Excesses"

Perhaps the greatest insight into the mind of history's most memorable and controversial figure can be found written in his own words, in the text of his autobiography, *My Best Excesses*. Published over the two-year period preceding his death, the original volume is approximated to be over 122,000 pages in length. However, during its first printing, Lord Dimwit frantically pulled roughly half of the pages from the press and had them sealed and buried four bloits underground, directly beneath the future site of his nine-bloit statue. The issue was, needless to say, not to be discussed within the court on punishment of gruesome execution, thus it can only be assumed that Dimwit got cold feet about publishing his more personal thoughts. Destroying such glorious prose as his own was certainly out of the question, so four bloits worth of dirt and sediment seemed the only rational solution.

Due to severe unfeasibility and general lack of interest, the missing text remained buried for over three centuries. But renewed interest in the Flathead Dynasty, sparked by the Grand Inquisitor's call for a return to Flathead values, generated the funding necessary to carry out the largest excavation ever undertaken. A team of scholars has spent the last seven years analyzing the unabridged work, splitting into groups of ten in order to scrutinize each chapter with the attention it demands, and gathering occasionally to discuss their many findings.

One of the most intriguing discoveries, thus far, has been the chapter in which Dimwit recounts the details of his heretofor unknown bout with the Famatharian Sniffles. In 765 GUE, during one of his extended summer vacations in the Eastlands (before becoming king and transporting the castle permanently), the future king took 6,000 of his closest friends on a camping trip in the forests of Famithria. After two months of "roughing it" in the wilderness, he suddenly developed an unremitting sneeze that forced him and his caravan to return home prematurely.

Dimwit Flathead spent the subsequent weeks strapped to his bed against his will. Though his retelling is quite certain on the matter, it is assumed that this was seen by all as the only possible way of preventing him from causing himself even greater suffering. He writes of his extreme longing to itch his nose, discussing in great detail the measures he wished to take in order to stop the relentless sensation, which included, among other things, the insertion of a fully grown porcupine into each nostril.

Though Prince Dimwit's behavior up until that point had always been seen as a bit excessive, history shows that his most stunning feats of overindulgence began immediately after this incident. Hundreds of pages of his autobiography were spent detailing the suffering he experienced, lying in that bed, unable to move his arms in the slightest, much less reach up and scratch his swollen, red nose.

The guards who stood watch outside his bedroom were made to pay dearly immediately following his recovery. In fact, some authors have suggested that the entire underground empire was made to pay for their collective unwillingness to let him scratch his proboscis.

THE WIZARD OF FROBOZZ

If fate turns as a wheel, then the court magician of Lord Dimwit, the Wizard of Frobozz, represents a low point for the excessive king. To see his beloved Castle Flathedia transformed into a pile of fudge would be too much for anyone to bear. Lord Dimwit, without giving so much as a written reprimand first, fired the Wizard. And without another thought, he ordered everyone anywhere to help rebuild the monument. Of course, the new castle would be 25 times larger than the previous one because Dimwit wanted it that way.

THE AGE OF GUILDS

With the public outcry that followed the Endless Fire, and Lord Dimwit's drastic response, the Enchanters' Guild found itself wielding more power than ever before. Each guild, whose elders comprised the Circle of Enchanters, was empowered to form schools for the training of new enchanters. This official sanctioning of the guilds led to the formation of numerous other chapters, with membership in excess of 2,000 by the year 800. The strength of the Enchanter's Guild was so great that it managed to outlast the empire's collapse and continue unchanged until 966. But that's a long way away.

THE CURSE OF MEGABOZZ

Lord Dimwit's incumbency was a 19 year stretch that, despite being full of surprises, became increasingly tiresome for the tormented commoners. In 789, after struggling to endure his mandated 98% taxation and fund his capricious whims for years, it was rumored that he was pondering an increase to a full 100% before the decade's end. Accompanied by the recent completion of his nine-bloit statue and the fact that it cast the entire town of Fublio in shadow, this was the last straw.

But it wasn't the disgruntled masses that dethroned and killed Dimwit. It was the temper of one particularly skilled wizard by the name of Megaboz. Appearing in the royal banquet hall on the 14th of Mumberbur in an explosion of billowing smoke, Megaboz uttered the historic words "No man, be he peasant or king, crosses Megaboz the Magnificent. Dimwit, thy kingship is a mockery of all worldly values! I curse your life! I curse your family! And I curse your Empire!" He then disappeared in a fiery explosion. Megaboz's curse took effect a few minutes later, with Dimwit's sudden and indisputable expiration, as well as the death of all 11 of Dimwit's siblings, but the remainder of the curse was delayed by the court magicians for 94 years.

The Flathead kings that followed after Dimwit were a panicky lot, each one trying harder than the last to remove the curse on the land. By the time the twelfth king of the condemned dynasty, Wurb Flathead, took the throne, the dreaded Curse Day was a mere two years away and the empire had already fallen into a completely frantic state over their impending doom. On the 14th of Mumberbur, 883, the empire collapsed. But not without one last valiant attempt at preventing its demise.

THE FIRST DUNGEON MASTER

During the final moments of the empire, a brave commoner came very close to preventing Megaboz from achieving his final goal. By assembling two items from each of the Twelve Flatheads, he came face to face with Megaboz and almost saved the kingdom, but alas, Megaboz's power was too great. Ironically, the commoner's attempt was rewarded by Megaboz himself. Sighting that the realm would need a guardian now that it had been sent into chaos, he dubbed the commoner Dungeon Master, giving him great magical powers, half the riches of the Flathead kingdom, and total dominion over the caverns of the Eastlands.

Following the events of Curse Day, entropy quickly took hold of the surface-world. Faced with the fact that Quendor was well past its prime, the once-great cities on both continents became dens of misery and confusion. But through it all, the tunnels and caves of the Eastlands remained stable under the watchful eye of the Dungeon Master. He guarded the many hidden entrances to the underground and allowed the fantastic assortment of mystical creatures within to roam freely. But in 948, he decided to make an exception.

THE LEGEND OF ZORK

The common folk-tale, known simply as the Legend of Zork, tells of an unknown adventurer who gained entrance into the underground empire through the mythical "White House," and began exploring the realm. In the process, the adventurer claimed the Twenty Treasures of Zork, defeated the Thief, the Wizard of Frobozz, and eventually met up with the Dungeon Master himself. As it turned out, the Dungeon Master had intentionally allowed the adventurer into his realm and was testing the adventurer's worthiness to take over the title. The adventurer passed the Dungeon Master's tests, and was anointed as the second Dungeon Master.

THE ALCHEMICAL DEBACLE

Elsewhere in the Eastlands, trouble was brewing in the form of four distinguished members of Quendorian society who had begun experimenting with the lost science of alchemy in an attempt to achieve immortality. To carry out their plan, they took the life of a young woman named Alexandria, much to the chagrin of her lover, who happened to be the son of one of the alchemists. As a result of their irresponsible misuse of alchemy's power, a dark force called the Nemesis was formed. This bitter spirit wandered the Eastlands, manifesting its anger by tormenting the scattered enclaves of society that occupied the regions near the four alchemists' homes. These areas were soon evacuated, and dubbed the Forbidden Lands by the Circle of Enchanters.

> *Note:* **For immediate history preceding Zork Grand Inquisitor, please refer to the chapter entitled "Backstory." It picks up shortly after this history leaves off.**

Footnotes

1. Unfortunately, I have not yet determined a way for adventurers to be able to read this text while standing in the darkest of dark places.

2. It is imperative that you read the text aloud. Otherwise it is certain to have no effect.

3. The languages of Borphee and Pheebor share the same roots. In the original dialect, only three different syllables were used, of which Bor and Phee are two. Common etiquette forbade the same syllable from being used more than once in any word. So the thousands of different expressions came entirely out of the inflection that was used to speak the 15 possible word combinations.

4. It was later discovered that Entharion had a working vocabulary of less than 75 words, and that his famous question was actually one of the most coherent sentences that he ever managed to complete.

5. Yoruk was never one for long-winded explanations. So when the Giant Coconut theory was explained to him, he apparently wasn't paying attention during the part about gravity.

6. This question, as well, has since been deemed silly.

7. It is not actually known if the Great Daemon of the Threshold had feet or, being a serpent-beast, balanced itself on a long, thick tail.

8. It is well documented, however, that Yoruk did indeed have feet.

9. As defined by the Encyclopedia Frobozzica, a bloit is equal to the distance that the king's favorite pet runs in an hour. This does, of course, change drastically from king to king and slightly from day to day, and is therefore an entirely useless form of measuement for most practical (and all historical) purposes.

CHAPTER VII:

A BRIEF HISTORY OF THE ZORK FRANCHISE

Long, long, ago (well, 20 years ago, or 160 dog years) in a galaxy far, far away, (well, that actually depends on how close you live to Boston) a Great Underground Empire was born. (Well, Underground in the sense of "basement," as in the basement of M.I.T.) Seven days after the release of *Star Wars*, (as Laird Malamed, Director of *Zork Grand Inquisitor*, likes to point out) the Zork Universe made a much quieter entrance into the twisted archive of Twentieth Century parallel universes.

ZORK I

What was finally published two years later, in 1979, as *Zork*, became not only the first of what has grown to be a series of nine Zork games (thirteen, if you count the related Enchanter trilogy and Wishbringer,) but one of the very first computer games ever published.

Zork seemed to develop naturally out of the earliest shareware text adventure game, Adventure, which already existed on many college mainframes at the time. *Zork* followed a fairly straightforward format, a treasure hunt throughout the Great Underground Empire for the Twenty Treasures, which the player collected inside the empty treasure case in the living room of the white house. *Zork* is, if not the first adventure game, often the first computer game many people remember playing.

Infocom is born

The founders of *Zork* ultimately started a game company to make more games. Infocom was christened in a small office in Cambridge, behind M.I.T. Their first task was to break up *Zork* into a trilogy (it was too big to fit on the truly floppy floppies available at the time). *Zork I* was published in 1981.

1981–Zork II: The Wizard of Frobozz

Months later, *Zork II* was released as a kind of text adventure add-on to *Zork I*, with the simple addition of more puzzles and new environments to explore, characters to interact with, including the blithering, incompetent Wizard of Frobozz. The off-beat, wacky Wizard was one of the first developed characters introduced in the Zork universe, and he more than anyone else established the witty, underground non-sensibility that was to become the classic trademark of the series.

1982–Zork III: The Dungeon Master

Zork III ends the opening trilogy of the Zork series, establishing the far end of a trajectory whereby the player has progressed in sophistication and knowledge to the point where the Dungeon Master names (you) as the successor to his high office of ruling wizard in the Underground, the Second Dungeon Master. It is presumably this Second Dungeon Master, or the Player of *Zork III*, who then hands the mantel off to Dalboz, just as magic disappears from the Empire, in *Zork Grand Inquisitor*. (If you can finish *Zork Grand Inquisitor*, then the Player again finds himself up for office in the line of succession to the Dungeon Mastership.)

1987–Beyond Zork

Beyond Zork is the story of the Player's quest to accumulate all the power of magic in Zork inside the Coconut of Quendor before it is to be banished from the Empire. This fourth text adventure is set in the same years as Infocom's related Enchanter Trilogy. *Beyond Zork* is unique among Zork games; released much later than the original Zork Trilogy, this text adventure attempts to be a text adventure version of a role playing game. In truth, Zork fans usually make fun of this title.

193

1988—ZORK ZERO

Zork Zero presented, like *Beyond Zork*, another ambitious departure from the simple parser text adventure format, this time in the form of an attempt to somehow integrate rudimentary graphical elements into the usual text adventure structure. The game was conceived as a prequel to *Zork I*, and meant to show the fall of the Great Underground Empire as a means of explaining why the environments of *Zork I*, *II*, and *III* had always seemed abandoned and eerie. By this time, however, the market for interactive fiction was flatter than a Flathead, and there would be no more text adventures based in Zork until the *Zork: The Undiscovered Underground* was released this year, in anticipation of *Zork Grand Inquisitor*.

1993—RETURN TO ZORK

Return to Zork represented a radical new direction for the franchise. Just as *Zork I* had taken the Adventure prototype and built it into a genre, so too did *Return to Zork* represent an ambitious leap into a previously untried medium—the CD-ROM. It is difficult to imagine that only four years ago, *Return to Zork* was one of the only games published for the CD-ROM. It also seems almost quaint, now, that *Return to Zork* was considered ground-breaking in its use of live actors (Jason Hervey (!) who, by the way, used to live one street up from me) and full motion video. *Return to Zork* celebrated the hallmark non-sensibility of the universe, and was perhaps the pivotal title that revitalized Activision into a major game company.

1996—Zork Nemesis

Sporting a new look and a new engine, *Zork Nemesis* marked the sophistication of the Zork franchise. The darkly inspired art design, with its immersive gothic sensibility, resulted in award-winning, pre-rendered art. The more sober sister of the previous Zork titles, *Zork Nemesis* became acclaimed for its complex characters, and involving, twisting story–a major accomplishment for what was essentially a non-linear, player-driven game. *Zork Nemesis* brought Zork to the global market, and Activision into the front pages of *Variety*, becoming one of the earliest Activision titles to be optioned for film development. (*Spycraft*, *Pitfall*, and *Interstate '76* have all followed suit.)

1997—Zork: The Undiscovered Underground

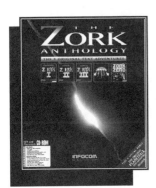

To mark the anniversary of Zork and to promote the new graphic adventure, *Zork Grand Inquisitor*, Activision commissioned two veterans of Infocom–Marc Blank (one of the M.I.T. students who started Zork) and Mike Berlyn–to write a new Zork text adventure. This chapter details the story of a minion of the Grand Inquisitor sent to investigate a new area of the underground. This (along with *Zork I - III*) is available for free at the Activision web site: www.activison.com.

1997—Zork Grand Inquisitor

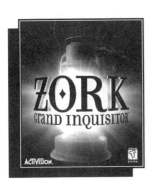

Lighter and more playful in both look and tone than *Zork Nemesis*, *Zork Grand Inquisitor* was conceived as an irreverent, slightly self-conscious adventure game. The title was designed as a kind of tribute to its 20-year history, and Activision has announced that ZGI is indeed only the first of a three part trilogy, just like *Zork I*, *II*, and *III*. Tentatively entitled the *Magic Wars Trilogy*, the three games are certain to focus on the war over magic within the Empire.

The Future of Zork

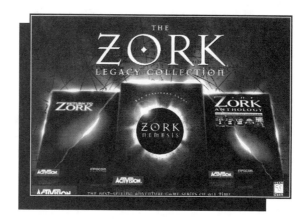

Just as the early Infocom Zork text adventures sought, time and again, a place for themselves in the changing platform of the PC, it is now Activision's turn to seek out a new place for the future worlds of Zork. Will Zork go 3-D? Will Zork become an Action/Adventure hybrid? Will there ever be a Zork console game (starring Bruce Willis?) Or will it simply fade away to Infocom heaven, like its sister universe, Planetfall?

My guess is, as long as there's granola left to mine, the Great Underground Empire will remain open for the plundering. That's just my opinion. You may think whatever you like. But in any case, take your old brass lantern with you.

You never know what's out there in the dark.

APPENDIX I
InvisiClues for Zork: The Undiscovered Adventure

Introduction

While making *Zork Grand Inquisitor*, Activision decided to commission the first new Zork text adventure in 10 years. Marc Blank and Mike Berlyn took up the challenge and created *Zork: The Undiscovered Underground*, which takes place the year before *Zork Grand Inquisitor*. The programming was done by Gerry Kevin Wilson, and Rich Lawrence and Stefan Jokisch provided WinFrotz as an engine.

The game itself can be downloaded for free from www.activision.com. Visit the *Zork Grand Inquisitor* area and navigate through the New Zork Hotel to the game room. (You can also download *Zork I, II* and *III* for free.)

In the spirit of the original Infocom text adventures, ZGI's director, Laird Malamed, wrote these InvisiClues to help players master *Zork: The Undiscovered Adventure*.

Factoid

InvisiClues were really just that—you would buy clues that came with an invisible ink pen, like the Yes & No books. The questions would be followed by a series of numbers. You rubbed the pen over the blank area and the clue appeared. We can't do that in this book, so you'll have to cover up the answers with your hand.

Q&A By Area

Entrance to the Undiscovered Underground

How do I shirk my responsibilities?

♦ Have you tried walking west?

♦ How about East?

♦ North, South, Down, Up?

♦ In other words, you can't. Type **Enter** or **NE** to go underground.

The boulders just collapsed my exit route. What do I do?

♦ You can try eating them.

♦ There's not much you can do with them at this point. You will need to get them removed to file your report though.

Convention Center

What's a Grue?

♦ The Grue is a sinister, lurking presence in dark places. Its favorite diet is adventurers, but its insatiable appetite is tampered by its fear of light. No Grue has ever been seen by the light of day, and few have survived its fearsome jaws to tell the tale.

How do I enter the Grues Convention with my lantern?

♦ Read the above description of Grues.

♦ They don't seem to like light, do they?

♦ Have you tried dropping your lantern?

♦ Of course, without your lamp, the Grues eat you.

♦ You cannot enter the convention with the lantern (on or off).

How do I survive in the Grue Convention?

♦ Without a light, you will have to rely on subterfuge.

♦ You will need to be in costume.

Where do I find a token for the Zork Underground Subway?

♦ In the bucket.

♦ At the bottom of the well.

♦ You know, just before the Dragon Stairs.

♦ What Subway?! This is not *Zork Grand Inquisitor*! This is one of those questions that was put in here for the sole purpose of teaching a lesson: Do not use the presence or absence of a question on a certain topic as an indication of what is important, and don't assume that long answers indicated important questions.

I'm hungry and I want a souvenir of my jaunt. How do I purchase items at the Souvenir Stand?

♦ Have you tried buying one?

♦ Don't have enough money, huh?

♦ What about taking one?

♦ The salesman doesn't seem to be into charity at the moment.

♦ You'll need to get rid of the salesman before you can obtain the candy or anything else at the Souvenir Stand.

How do I chase away the salesman?

♦ He looks kind of creepy, don't you think?

♦ Why would his face be so unmoving—it isn't natural.

♦ Maybe that's not his face!

♦ Have you spoken to him yet?

♦ He's wearing a mask. You need to remove it.

How do I take the mask off the salesman?

♦ He's pretty well out of reach behind the counter.

♦ You'll need to get him to come closer.

♦ Type "Salesman, hello" or "Talk to salesman" to get him to lean forward, then take his mask. Be sure to read the description carefully.

Am I mistaken, or did the game just describe a Grue?

♦ Pretty sacrilegious, huh?

♦ Didn't think that was coming, did you?

- We're pretty proud of ourselves for taking that chance.
- Well, it wasn't that big a chance as we had Marc Blank and Mike Berlyn write the game.

Was that the first time a Grue was described in a Zork game?

- Of course. Everything in this game is brand, spanking new.
- Well, except for Grues.
- And Zork.
- And the lantern.
- Now that you mention it, you can Frotz a Grue in Sorcerer anytime you are in the dark to get a brief description of these fearsome creatures.

What can I do with the popcorn?

- You can string it together for a decoration.
- How about shipping your computer to mom?
- Maybe soak up a small reservoir?
- All you can do with it is eat it.

What do I do with the masks, gloves, and body suits in the Changing Room?

- You could wear them.
- Do you see any items that resemble any of the local wildlife?
- Which ones make up the best Grue disguise?
- Note the look of the Grue Salesman when you take off his mask. Then wear the same items to dress up like a Grue.

How do I survive the Grue Convention?

- Your costume only fools the Grues for so long. You can't survive more than a few moves.

After jumping down the chute, how do I stop the walls from collapsing in the Trash Compactor?

- Have you braced the walls with the pole?
- Did you shoot the snake creature in the water?

♦ Have you tried a laser blaster on the door?

♦ What trash compactor? There is no way to survive jumping down the chute.

Why do I want to go in the convention anyway?

♦ You need to grab the glasses.

THEATER

How do I navigate the maze of seats?

♦ Don't you love mazes?

♦ This one is huge.

♦ Did you try dropping objects in each of the environments and then mapping the areas?

♦ Wow, you could walk for days.

♦ Better yet, don't bother. There is no way to get through the maze. It only exists to teach you not to go into mazes.

How do I take a lens off a footlight?

♦ They are hot to the touch.

♦ You need something to protect your hands.

♦ Wear any of the gloves from the Changing Room.

What's in the trunk?

♦ Why don't you open it?

HALL OF SCIENCE

How do I raise the cover and push the button?

♦ That cover is pretty heavy. You need to keep holding it with one hand.

♦ It takes another hand to push the button.

♦ You need to drop all of your inventory you are carrying to open the cover and push the button.

♦ You do not need to drop items you are wearing.

How do I see the image under the cover?

♦ The image is fuzzy and out of alignment.

♦ Did you notice the colors?

♦ You will need special eye wear to correct the image.

♦ What about the lenses?

♦ Put the red and blue lenses in the glasses.

♦ Wear the glasses, raise the cover and push the button.

How do I get through the sealed door?

♦ You need to align the symbols on the floor.

♦ Did you look at the image under the cover?

♦ Place the models on the correct symbols to unlock the door.

Where do I find a second Five Zorkmid coin?

♦ Did you check the trunk for a second coin?

♦ Did you look under all the seats?

♦ Maybe you should steal one from the Grues?

♦ Of course, that would all be too easy.

♦ There is only one Five Zorkmid coin.

How do I consult the oracle with only five Zorkmids?

♦ You need a way to make your money last.

♦ Did you look at the coin?

♦ Interesting shape, isn't it?

♦ You could try to attach something to the coin so you can retrieve it.

♦ TIE THE TINSEL TO THE COIN. You can now insert the coin twice.

How do I open the Janitor's Closet?

♦ Did you Rezrov the door?

♦ Whoops, wrong game again. Maybe something else will work?

♦ How about a skeleton key?

♦ Actually, the skeleton is the key to this puzzle.

♦ Consult the Oracle in the Museum of Illusions for more information.

THE CAGE

How do I survive the Rat-Ants?

♦ They are pretty hungry.

♦ Maybe you could feed them.

♦ Hey, they like candy?

♦ Is there anything else sweet around that could curb their appetite?

♦ The boulders blocking your escape are sweet.

How do I get the Rat-Ants to the Tunnel?

♦ They are not very smart.

♦ And they like candy.

♦ Maybe you could lure them to the tunnel.

♦ Leave a trail of candy between the Cage and the Cultural Complex.

I escaped, but so did the Rat-Ants.

♦ You need to arm yourself with a deterrent before you make your escape.

♦ Did you know that Rat-Ants are insects, not rodents?

♦ Make sure you have the Bug Spray before you lead the Rat-Ants to the outside.

♦ Oh yeah, make sure you don't waste the spray before then either.

GENERAL QUESTIONS

How do I turn the lantern on?

♦ Did you read the description of the Lantern?

♦ Looks to be in bad shape.

♦ The switch doesn't seem to work.

♦ If you were really frustrated with a device, what would you do?

♦ HIT THE LANTERN to turn it back on.

Where do I get some tinsel?

♦ Where do you usually find tinsel?

♦ Are there any trees around?

♦ Look at the miniature tree in the Mud Forum.

What do I do with the bug spray?

♦ You kill bugs of course, but only at the right time.

How Points Are Scored

Points Awarded:	Action:
5	*Fixing the lantern*
8	*Seeing a Grue*
10	*Impersonating a Grue*
5	*Opening the massive door*
5	*Choosing a lens*
5	*Experimenting with the glasses*
10	*Revealing the hidden picture*
8	*Decorating a coin*
10	*Consulting the oracles*
5	*Opening the closet*
19	*Finding sundry items*
5	*Escaping the GUE*
5	*Debugging the GUE*
(100 Total)	

For Your Amusement—have you tried...

♦ Attempting to kill the Salesman?

♦ Breaking the Mirror in the Changing Room?

♦ Going down the Trash Chute?

♦ Wearing the adventurer's hat from the Convention Hall?

♦ Licking the Boulders?

♦ Sitting on the seats in the Theater main area?

♦ Looking at the curtains?

♦ Pulling down the curtains?

♦ Taking a bow on stage?

♦ Looking at the stickers on the trunk?

APPENDIX II
OBJECTS IN ZORK GRAND INQUISITOR

Object Name:	Where Found:	Where Used:
Perma-Suck Machine	Beginning Inventory	GUE Tech Rotunda
Noose/Rope	Frobozz Electric HQ Ext.	Well; Monastery Subway
Plastic Soda Can Holder	Foozle Fish Market	Foozle Dock
Can of Mead	Foozle Fish Market	Dungeon Master Garden
Broken Lantern	Foozle Dock	Jack's Pawn Shop
Auto Lighting Cigar	Jack's Pawn Shop	Foozle Street; Dungeon Master Garden
Working Lantern	Jack's Pawn Shop	Throughout the game
Spell Book	Given by Y'Gael	Throughout the game
Subway Token	Well Bottom	Crossroads; Subway Entrance
Small Hammer	Crossroads Emergency Case	Crossroads; Garden
Sword	Crossroads Emergency Case	Crossroads; Dungeon Master Garden; Spell Press Labs; Monastery Subway; Mesa

Object Name:	Where Found:	Where Used:
Map	Crossroads Emergency Case	Crossroads; Spell Press Labs; GUE Tech Exterior; Dungeon Master Garden; Monastery Subway; Hades
Shovel	Dungeon Master Garden	GUE Tech Exterior
Snap Dragon	Dungeon Master Garden	Dungeon Master Garden
Honey	Dungeon Master Garden	Dungeon Master Vista Room
Fudge	Dungeon Master Vista Room	Dungeon Master Vista Room
Hotbugs	Dungeon Master Vista Room	Dungeon Master Vista Room
Mug	Dungeon Master Vista Room	Dungeon Master Vista Room
Hungus Lard	Dungeon Master Vista Room	Dungeon Master Garden
SNA scroll piece	Dungeon Master Mirror Room	Inventory
VIG scroll piece	Dungeon Master Wardrobe Room	Inventory
Ripped Snavig Scroll	Made in Inventory	Spell Press Labs
Zorkmids	Change from Zorkmid Bill	GUE Tech Rotunda; Flood Control Dam #3; Hades
Zork Rocks	GUE Tech Rotunda	Infinite Corridor
Ice Cream Sandwich	GUE Tech Rotunda	Melts into Obidil Scroll

Appendix II: Objects in Zork Grand Inquisitor

Object Name:	Where Found:	Where Used:
Obidil Scroll	GUE Tech Rotunda	Spell Press Labs
ProZork Pill	Infinite Corridor	Dungeon Master Garden
Student ID	Infinite Corridor	Infinite Corridor
Blank Beburtt Scroll	Spell Press	Labs
Letter Opener	Made in FCD Subway	Inventory
Lottery Ticket	Hades Subway Station	Inventory
500 Zorkmid Bill	Winning Old Scratch Lottery	GUE Tech Rotunda
Griff Totem	Crossroads	Throughout the Game
Brog Totem	Hades	Throughout the Game
Lucy Totem	Perils of Magic Exhibit	Throughout the Game
Sword and Rope	Combined in Inventory	Monastery Subway
Teletype Hammer	Frobozz Electric Exterior	Perils of Magic Exhibit
Totemizer Warning	Jail	Jail
Key	Jail	Jail
Playing Cards	Jack's Bar	Jack's Bar
Cube of Foundation	Strip Room	Radio Tower
Mail it to Hades Envelope	White House Mailbox	Inventory
Bickering Torch	White House Exterior	Not Used

Object Name:	Where Found:	Where Used:
Flickering Torch	*White House Exterior*	*Grue's Lair*
Wooden Board	*White House Exterior*	*Grue's Lair*
Grue's Egg	*Grue's Lair*	*Grue's Lair*
Hard boiled Egg	*Made in Camp Fire*	*Grue's Lair*
Rocks	*Grue's Lair*	*Eaten by Brog*
Skull of Yoruk	*Grue's Lair*	*Radio Tower*
Inflatable Sea Captain	*Dragon Islands*	*Dragon Islands*
Inflatable Raft	*Dragon Islands*	*Dragon Islands*
Air Pump	*Dragon Islands*	*Dragon Islands*
Dragon Tooth	*Dragon's Mouth*	*Dragon's Nose*
Rope	*Dragon's Mouth*	*Dragon Islands*
Coconut of Quendor	*Dragon's Mouth*	*Radio Tower*

APPENDIX II: OBJECTS IN ZORK GRAND INQUISITOR

APPENDIX III
SPELLS IN ZORK GRAND INQUISITOR

LEGEND:

S.P.L. = SPELL PRESS LABS

Spell Types:

H = HIGH

M = MIDDLE

D = DEEP

SPELL NAME:	WHERE FOUND:	WHERE USED:	SPELL TYPE:
Beburtt	Created in GUE Tech S.P.L.	Crossroads	H
Booznik Scroll	Given by Y'Gael	Spellbook	D
Dratsay	Created in Booznik Reversal	Not Used	M
Eliwran	Created in Booznik Reversal	Not Used	M
Frolg	Created in Booznik Reversal	Not Used	D
Givans	Created in Booznik Reversal	Not Used	N/A
Glorf	White House Exterior	Well Bottom	D
Golgatem	FCD Subway Station	GUE Tech S.P.L.	H
Igram	In Spellbook	GUE Tech Rotunda	D
Kcorht	Created in Booznik Reversal	Not Used	D
Kendall	GUE Tech Exterior Dirt Pile	Crossroads Subway; Hades; Infinite Corridor	M
Lexdum Scroll	Given by Jack	Jail	M
Lidibo	Created in Booznik Reversal	Not Used	H
Lladnek	Created in Booznik Reversal	Not Used	M

Spell Name:	Where Found:	Where Used:	Spell Type:
Margi	Created in Booznik Reversal	Mesa	D
Maxov	Created in Booznik Reversal	Radio Tower	H
Metaglog	Created in Booznik Reversal	Not Used	H
Narwile	Castle Interior	Dungeon Master Wardrobe Room; Hades; Perils of Magic Exhibit	M
Obidil	GUE Tech Ice Cream Machine	Dungeon Master Vista Room	H
Rezrov	In Spellbook	Well Bottom; Crossroads; Flood Control Dam	M
Snavig	Dungeon Master Wardrobe Room Dungeon Master Mirror Room	Hades	D
Throck	Dungeon Master Garden Shed	Dungeon Master Garden; FCD Subway	D
Ttrubeb	Created in Booznik Reversal	Not Used	H
Vorzer	Created in Booznik Reversal	Mesa	M
Voxam	In Spellbook	Not Used	H
Yastard	Given by Dungeon Master	Dungeon Master Wardrobe Room; Hades; Perils of Magic Exhibit	M
Zimdor Scroll	Crossroads Umbrella Tree	Dungeon Master Garden	D

Index